I0156071

As you grow into adulthood,
life will bring you many
amazing experiences.

To:

With Love, From:

"Adulthood is not an age, but a stage of
knowledge of oneself." ~ John Fowles

HELP

THE ALL-IN-ONE RESOURCE FOR TEENS, PREFLIGHTS, AND NEETS TO MASTER THE BASICS OF LIFE SKILLS

PERSONAL DEVELOPMENT

MENTAL

SOCIAL

EMOTIONAL

SPIRITUAL

PHYSICAL

SYDNEY BROWN

PART OF THE SOCIAL STAMINA SERIES

HELP

THE ALL-IN-ONE RESOURCE FOR TEENS, PREFLIGHTS, AND NEETS TO MASTER THE BASICS OF LIFE SKILLS

© Copyright 2023 by Sydney Brown. All rights reserved.

Hardcover 978-1-959948-00-1
Paperback 978-1-959948-03-2
eBook 978-1-959948-04-9

No part of this publication may be reproduced, distributed, or transmitted in any form or by any means, including photocopying, recording, or other electronic or mechanical methods, without the prior written permission of the publisher, except in the case of brief quotations embodied in critical reviews and specific other noncommercial uses permitted by copyright law.

Disclaimer: *The information presented is the author's opinion and does not constitute health or medical advice. The content of this book is for informational purposes only and is not intended to diagnose, treat, cure, or prevent any condition or disease. This book is designed for the readers' information only. While every effort was made to ensure the accuracy and effectiveness of the tips and guides, the author does not guarantee that everything will work in all types of scenarios. For Please practice vigilance and safety for skills that need expertise and pretty dangerous in; please consult with a professional. For health-related matters, it would be best to consult a healthcare professional.*

The reader accepts that the author is not responsible for any action or effect that results from reading and application of the content in this book.

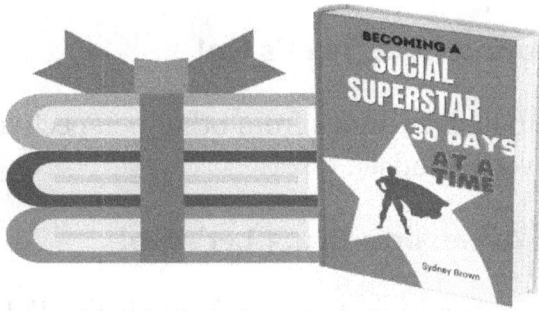

Get Your Free Gift!

Do you feel like it's time for a change?

Are you considering moving out? Or are your parents dropping a few too many hints, grab a free 30-day planner to organize your life so you can get a plan together for whatever upcoming goals you have!

With this, you can keep track of:

30 DAY CHALLENGE

- MONTHLY BUDGET
- WEEKLY MEAL PLANNER
- WEEKLY PLANNER
- DAILY GRATITUDE LIST
- DAILY TO-DO LIST
- DAILY SCHEDULE
- DAILY JOURNAL

Go now to https://www.dontstopuntil.com/30d-ss-getyourplanner (Yes! It's totally FREE!)

TLM Publishing House

Social Stamina – 1,2,3 Let's Go!

Titles to help look at things from other perspectives and strengthen your mindset.

The Great Ascension–1,2,3 Let's Go!

Titles to help you gain focus and climb the ladder of success!

How to Start – 1,2,3 Let's Go!

Titles to help you with step-by-step, must-have knowledge of the business world and personal experiences.

Top 10 Questions to Ask Before You...1,2,3 Let's Go!

Titles with must-have questions (and logic behind) for many of life's daily and significant decisions.

Social Media

Facebook: facebook.com/tlmpublishinghouse

Website: www.TTpublishinghouse.com

Dedication

Some people are happy just existing and having things dropped in their laps. Sure, it may be simpler, but those who stay hidden away miss out on such a great world on the other side of the door.

Then some can't wait to leave home and flee as quickly as possible. This may work for some, but for others, it could be catastrophic, if unprepared

And just like Goldilocks and the Three Bears, some make a decision that's their own *Just Right* path. They make a life they can find happiness in today and prepare for their future by learning things that help them become self-sufficient.

They don't want to rush out before it's time, but they make sure they have the emotional and physical survival skills for everyday living. That way, when they are ready to take flight into adulthood, they're ready to grow and thrive in life.

I don't believe you're one of the people who live in fear. I believe you are special and will learn, grow, and prepare for your future, goals, and dreams!

If you're ready to move to the next phase of Life Skills – This book is dedicated to you.

Preface

When I look back to the years when I was younger, I see the meek, insecure, lost, and confused young woman I used to be. She was living for the day she could be a grown-up and live independently.

All her young life was spent wanting to be able to make independent, adult decisions. Then, when she was out there, all she could think of was how she should have prepared a bit better.

I've failed so many times in life, whether business or personal, that people who never ventured outside their comfort zone would sit and judge me as a failure. But, I chose to step outside of my comfort zone and reached toward the next step and then the next. Eventually, I made it to a point where I felt confident and competent enough to help others avoid the same messes that life can throw at you.

As you read this book, I want you to imagine it's written specifically for you, by a big sister who wants great things for you... because it is. When I was just a small child, I grew up in "Foster Care."

I was lucky because I stayed with the same family most of my life and they treated me as their own. But there's always a little voice in the back of your head that wonders if this is the day that I have to pack a bag and move to a different home.

I hope you haven't had this experience, but if you have, please know there is a great life ahead of you.

If I say something that sounds like I'm talking down to you, keep in mind that I'm writing this for people from ages thirteen to about twenty-six, so I write to a broad group of readers. Here are just a few of the potential readers who could really benefit from having this book on your shelf as a handy reference.

- Teen (13-17)
- Young adult (17+)
- Preflight (18+ -- getting ready to Fly the Coop or Leave the Nest)
- NEET (Not Engaged in Education, Employment, or Training)
- Any adult who may have 'missed the memo'!

Whether you consider yourself to have more or fewer obstacles than others, trust me, we all have our own personal battles. I encourage people who are in different spots on the spectrum to learn as they can. We've added some handy graphics to help visual learners as well. There are warning areas that you want to pay attention to. Safety is always a priority, whether you're in your home or outside it.

You may not be familiar with the NEET term yet. Some consider NEET to be another word for what used to be called "late bloomer", and to some, it's regarded as an insult. If you consider yourself a NEET and are not sure this book is for you, I encourage you to keep it handy and read it because sometimes you may find your belly growling and there's no one to whip up a meal for you.

I assure you, as a self-identified late bloomer, I rushed out of the home, but it took me quite a bit longer to feel like I could survive on my own. I offer zero judgment, only understanding, and a hand up toward your next phase.

Let's get your Life Skills List growing.

About the Author

Sydney Brown has spent over thirty-five years in the business world and later in the corporate world. She has learned what works and what doesn't when the goal is to get out of the stale, vanilla world of the generations before us.

She believes that each person has at least one successful business, one book, and one grand adventure in them, but most people don't know how to figure out their best fit, so they stay where they are.

She has an honorary *Doctor of Philosophy* in *Human Services* from Provident University due to her passion for helping others find their best lives. She is a best-selling author, speaker, and coach, helping people reach out of their current situation and reinvent themselves so they can do more than exist and survive while in this great space.

Personally, she's a mom of two adulting children and proudly owns the title of "Crazy Cat Lady" among her friends. After too many years of avoiding *living* life, she is on a mission to help others identify and begin their own "Great Ascension."

She can be found at https://www.justsydneybrown.com and across social media at JustSydneyBrown as well.

H
HOUSEKEEPING, MAINTENANCE & COOKING

E
EMOTIONAL MANAGEMENT SKILLS

L
LIFE & PRACTICAL SKILLS

P
PERSONAL DEVELOPMENT LIFE SKILLS

CONTENTS

Contents

Disclaimer & Safety Precautions

Utmost effort has been done to ensure that this book is helpful for all readers. However, like most instructional and self-help books, there are some limitations to the scope of entries or procedures found here.

People who have injuries or have had medical procedures, and people with disabilities may have some difficulties with a few of the tasks, so assistance in doing the tasks is highly encouraged to avoid any accidents. A reminder or tips are placed at the bottom of each applicable section that people who are injured or with a disability may find helpful. Please understand if some procedures seem too basic since we aim to ensure that everyone is given equal opportunities to do the tasks and that those who are not yet familiar with the tasks can follow the instructions.

Not all instructions or procedures are fool proof. Some may not work properly depending on the different factors surrounding the tasks. You may check with your parents or ask proper people with expertise on the subject matter for help online if you feel that the procedures found here do not fully answer your needs and requirements. Some instructions, if not done correctly, may result in injury or property loss; utmost care is required to do any of the tasks that require unique know-how. Do not proceed if you feel there may be a resulting danger or risk while doing the tasks.

Ensure that you don't have any allergies and test for possible chemical reactions first before doing anything dangerous. Do not ingest food if you're not sure you're allergic to it. Supervision by adults and professionals may be required for certain tasks and circumstances.

Your health and safety should always be the top priority.

Introduction

Woot! Woot!

Are you (or somebody you care about) a new teenager who's ready to take on the world head-first?

Maybe you're well into your teen years, and facing the nerves that come with preparing to go out into your new life of 'adulting' and all that goes with it?

Or maybe you're happy to be right where you are, and have no interest in leaving, but do need to know some of the necessities of survival should you find no dinner on the table when your belly starts to growl...

This book will help you learn to:
- Perform some of the basics of life that they just don't teach in school anymore: like how to sew on a button or change a flat tire, or even prepare a budget.

- Identify the things that you may not have thought of otherwise, so you are prepared to manage things and cope with situations without panicking.

- Strengthen your mindset so that when times get tough, you'll be tougher!

If you're looking for the perfect gift for your:

- Teen (13-17)
- Young adult (17+)
- Preflight (18+ -- getting ready to Fly the Coop or Leave the Nest)
- NEET (Not Engaged in Education, Employment, or Training)
- Any adult who may have 'missed the memo'!

Life skills are important, but until you need them, you may have missed the memo entirely! Keep this book handy and you'll learn things that they probably don't teach you in school anymore!

LIVING WITH PARENTS

Living with your parents can be easy and difficult at the same time. It's easy because parents provide for us, care for us, and they always look out for us.

Living with them can also be tough because there will always be a time when they cannot understand us. They would often seem to get in the way of our happiness. That is why most of us have experienced rebelling against our parents at some point in our lives.

Yes, there will be conflict, but we should not forget that our parents love us. We are all aware that the reason why there are house rules is that they want to protect us.

There might be instances where our parents would look overprotective and strict, but they do it for our sake.

When parents teach you or ask you to do household chores, they are not doing it to order you around. They are not doing it to "ruin your life." They are teaching you important life skills.

You'll realize that these skills are important as you venture out on your own. So, pause your favorite console, game, app, or whatever it is you're doing online. Learn and appreciate the life skills that you're being taught.

The next time your parents ask you to do household chores, do it not for them, but for your sake. Try to consider it on the job training. That's right, no grumbling and complaining!

When you're on your own, that's when you'll likely realize and thank them for what they've taught you.

Not all parents are equally available. Some may be too busy to teach all the skills you need out in the world. Try to understand, they're not trying to neglect your basic education. They're busy earning money to provide for the family and unfortunately, many in recent generations haven't had the time to dig into these types of skills. Try to appreciate what they're able to do. Many others aren't as lucky, though it may not seem like luck to you at the moment.

Sometimes, it's up to you to teach yourself some of the life skills you need. That's why we came up with this book.

Pros And Cons of Living with Your Parents

➕ ADVANTAGES	➖ DISADVANTAGES
• Save Money. • Help with household chores. • Someone will cook for you. • Someone can take care of you. • Someone will wake you up. • More family bonding moments. • Someone is to support you. • Study without worrying. • Parents can teach you more life skills.	• Little or no private space. • No hosting of house parties unless approved by parents. • Unsolicited advice and clash with your parents. • Others may think less of you. • Hard to maintain a love life and relationships. • Delay in property investment.

Living with your parents has its perks as well as disadvantages. This list will help you become more appreciative of your situation. It will also highlight the things you're taking for granted.

It can also help you realize what you'll be getting if you're going to start living on your own. So, learn all the necessary life skills you'll get from your parents by reading this book.

Let's face it, regardless of how you feel overall, there are good things and bad things associated with having parents! Sadly, most of us grow up anxious to get out of the home or hating our parents for one reason or another. Then one day, you realize that your parents weren't the idiots you were convinced they were back when you were still home.

For some, that day of revelation comes before they've even moved out, but for all too many, we don't realize how much your parents did to protect and guide you toward a great future. Often when you figure it out, it's too late to tell them that you realize it now.

This book is for *you*, not your parents. But that said, if I could have one wish, since I've lived both sides and learned the hard lessons, I would wish that you recognize that you parent(s) are people *and* parents.

They're doing the best they can. Some people got put in a family with parents who are struggling to just barely hold it together. Others may have a perfect life (from the outside, but there are still pressures and issues that they have to overcome).

Once you recognize them as people, and not just parents, it might help you recognize that they're just trying to do the best they can with what they know. You may not respect their actions, and some may not even be safe around them, but try to forgive them for being human beings who are far from perfect but doing their best.

I could say you should realize how lucky you are to be living with your parents. Maybe you already are. But I don't know your situation. I grew up in foster care, so my biological mother was pretty messed up.

It took some time, but I was able to understand that no one guided her through how to live a better life. No one showed her how to be a good mom. So, she messed up a lot of things...a LOT! But today, I recognize that she didn't hurt us on purpose. She just didn't know how to do better.

That's truly one of the main reasons I'm writing this book! We have to make sure that each generation takes the time to look at the good with the bad. Look around your home and your daily life. Figure out what you want to do "just like Mom did it" but also recognize the things that you are sure you want to do "any way other than Mom did it."

I'm confident your parents will be glad that you learn from their mistakes if you do something different than the way they handled things. But, try to be logical and remove the anger when you make this list in your head.

You may find your parents aren't as bad as you thought. You may even gain a level of appreciation for their efforts, even if they fall short of the goal. This appreciation should translate to more respect for them.

You are the only one who can determine if you will be an angsty young adult who puts off doing your share of the work until someone forces you to contribute. I'm going to suggest you do it without the battle. It'll be easier on you both, and you'll likely realize that the chores aren't as bad as it may seem.

Pros

Joint Contributions: Money & Chores

You could save money when living with your parents. Living by yourself, you'd worry about rent, household expenses, utility bills, and all that goes with it.

That doesn't mean you can hide out in your room until you inherit the family home. Most parents assign age-appropriate chores to contribute and teach you responsibility. No, they didn't have you just so they could make you do all the work.

In any healthy relationship, there should be give and take. If they're paying the bills, you should be willing to help with keeping the home clean and other chores as needed.

If you don't have a job right now, it would be logical to expect you to do more of the cooking and cleaning and other chores than even your parents. It's your contribution. Theirs is paying the bills.

If you do have a job, there may be a rent/housing that your parents charge you. This isn't to make money off you, but to make sure that you are learning responsibility and not taking advantage of the situation. If you're ten, no one expects you to pay toward housing. If you're seventeen or older, it becomes something that's more common.

Many parents offer their young adult children to stay for free while they work or attend school, but if they're legally an adult, they may find it's time to renegotiate. Don't be mad at them. They're trying to help you take the next steps toward adulting on your own.

Nurse/Caregiver

When you're sick, if you're like the rest of us, you probably want someone to come and check on you, bring you a cool cloth for your forehead, and maybe some chicken noodle soup.

If you're living on your own, you may not have a choice, but to nurse yourself back to health. Times like this make even the most mature adulting child miss his mom and her genuine love and concern.

That doesn't mean you should just stay living with your parents forever, just to have someone to take care of you, but if you do, try to remember to say thanks.

Built-in Cook

Cooking is one of those life skills that you can learn enough to survive in a very short time. But to truly become good at it, takes some people a lifetime to master. So, keep in mind, each meal your parents set at the table for you (or wherever your family eats), the life cycle of a meal isn't always easy.

For fun, let's trace it back. You have a homecooked meal in front of you. Let's say it's a chicken breast, mashed potatoes and mixed vegetables. You probably have some sort of beverage as well.

So, look at each thing on your plate. The chicken breast was probably bought packaged, but there was likely some sort of marinade, or some sort of time involved in preparation.

Then they had to have taken the time to plan the seasonings for the chicken. The mashed potatoes took time to peel, cube, boil, then mash or whip them just the way you like them, whether with milk, cream, butter, or a special mixture of all.

Your mixed vegetables may have come out of a bag or a can, but someone had to plan ahead and buy those. If they're truly homemade, they went to the grocery store in recent enough days so that they could buy the vegetables in the fresh produce section, then had to make sure they timed the meal properly so the veggies wouldn't go bad and need to be thrown out. They likely had to peel or chop, slice, or dice them before cooking.

Then there's probably a salad that needed to be bought from the produce section and all cleaned, cut or pulled, and then of course, they had to remember to get everyone's favorite salad dressings or make theirs homemade as well.

Let's be real... if you have someone cooking this type of homemade meal for you, you probably never want to move out! Heck, I may want to come and stay with your family too!

Being your own cook can be one of the most intimidating roles of adulting. Cooking is a skill that requires years of practice. While you're with your parents, let them teach you the secret family recipes. Those will be an emotional goldmine in the future.

A Helper

If you've ever overslept or snoozed your alarm and missed something important, you probably can appreciate the fact that having a parent around to yell at you to push some of the adrenaline in your system, may actually be helpful.

Sometimes you might sleep heavily or may not be getting enough sleep. The fact that you know you can rely on your parent to wake you may also help you sleep more soundly.

Make sure before you move out, that you've trained yourself to be responsible enough to drag yourself out of bed when your alarm goes off. It's one of those things that people rarely even give a second thought about, until they miss a big job interview or end up late for an important meeting at work.

Sometimes just having someone around to listen to how your day went, can make the difference between a bad or a good day.

Memory Makers

Time is the one resource in the world that's irreplaceable. Time with your parents is very important. We're all growing older and before you know it, it's time to move out and be more independent.

We don't know when we'll be able to bond and have fun moments with our parents since moving out means less family time. Believe me, movie or Netflix nights, sports, picnics, etc. are precious. You'll look back at those moments as your happiest because you're with your parents.

Living with your parents makes it easier to build a stronger bond with them. You don't have to travel far or schedule anything to enjoy time with them, the only thing needed is that you go home.

Support System

Your greatest fans and supporters are likely your parents. They give advice, hear you out, and can be your BFF when you're feeling down. Living with your parents makes it easier to run to their arms and destress.

Did you have a breakup with someone? Or get in a fight at school? Your parents will likely struggle to put on their parenting hat at times when you're hurting or angry, because seeing you struggling hurts them too.

Ultimately, they likely will take a breath and calm themselves down, so they can offer suggestions to you. Or, in cases where they just don't know what the right answer is, they may just put an arm around you and just be there with you.

Teachers by Example

Having a parent or two to teach you valuable life skills is the cherry on top of the cake. Life skills are best taught by your parents. They have their personal experiences that they can impart to you. This would make each lesson more special and memorable. You may not realize it now, but every day has the potential for becoming one of your favorite memories with your parent. Don't block the potential with a bad attitude.

Cons

If there are pros, surely there are also cons of living with your parents. These may be the reasons that will push you in the future to seek a place of your own.

Privacy

Parents can be a little nosy at times. They may poke around in your room when you're not there, or maybe they're just always there, especially after the pandemic. This leaves you with little to no private space. Yes, your room is where you go to be alone, but if you're living with your parents, there are certain rules that you still need to follow.

They may not let certain friends over or not allow the opposite gender in your room. Bottom line, their house, their rules. This is one of the main reasons teens who want to make their own decisions and have their own space decide it's time to move out.

Living with your parents means that you need to ask for your parents' permission on pretty much anything you do. This includes parties. Talk about a downer if you're trying to get in with a certain group at school!

Differences of Opinion

Parents are good at giving advice. You may or may not have asked for it, but trust me, they'll let you know if they see any red flags. These opinions or advice may lead to arguments. Since they're your parents, they'll notice your issues and problems. Sometimes, even if you want them to mind their own business, they'd still press on you to give them details. They may be nosy but that's because they care.

Other Opinions

I can still recall a conversation I had with a friend back in high school where we were complaining about how much we hated our parents. They make us come home too early. They want to see who we're dating. They're essentially running our lives—so how will we ever escape? We'd all agreed we'd get apartments together or go to school together and get out of the house as soon as possible.

So, what happens if you're okay with the rules your parents set for you and you're not in a rush to turn 18 and escape? If you replay the conversation above but imagine that you're one of the people in the conversation. If you told the others, "Nah, I'm cool at home. Three hots and a cot there is better than somewhere else!"

Your friends may look at you like you had two heads! Sometimes you might just say the same thing as others, just to stay part of the group.

This is another example of how you are who you spend time with. If your friends were all saying how much they loved having a hot dinner every night and then TV time with the family, it's logical that it might rub off onto you as well. So, if you want to stay at home later than your friends, be bold in your feelings and talk with your parents about it.

No matter what your reason is for still living with your parents, don't mind what others think.

Love and relationships.

Your parents may seem overly protective. Try to remember, you're their baby, even if you're thirty or forty. They may cross boundaries you try to set because they feel that you're still "their baby" and they want to protect you. For better or worse, that will likely never go away. You'll appreciate it eventually.

Late Bloomers

One of the major concerns about living with your parents is that if you're living off your parent's income, you may not be earning, saving, building your own credit, or investing toward your own future.

This may be seen as a problem because traditionally the cost of properties rises. The longer into your life before you invest, you may be short-changing yourself some years of building equity in a property.

This may be the case for some. For others, the opportunity of living with their parents is a way of saving faster to buy properties. This is because they have fewer expenses to think about and have more money to invest. Setting up and living on your own is a big decision. You can do this once you have all the right life skills. In time, you'll become more stable with your emotions and finances. While you're still living with your parents, earn your keep.

Respect

We respect our teachers in school because they're the ones who teach and guide us while we learn in school.

Some of us forget that our parents are our first teachers. They teach us good manners and life skills that we don't learn in school. They too, deserve our respect.

Your parents may seem to be strict and have endless house rules but remember that these are all for your sake. Our parents love us and only want the best for us, so the very least we can do for them is to give them the respect they deserve.

For most people, it takes the death or loss of a parent or both parents for us to appreciate and respect them. Don't let this happen to you.

Go ahead and tell your parents how much you love and respect them. Do it now because tomorrow is not promised.

Remember to show your respect and appreciation while they are still present in your life.

"I respect my parents, but I don't know why they think I'm disrespecting them."

Is this familiar? Your parents have a different mindset. What seems okay with you may be offensive to them and vice-versa. You might call it old fashioned, but they grew up in a time where people didn't call each other the same slang names you might. I can remember the first time I called my dad "Dude"... and I had a cool dad, but he looked at me, one eyebrow raised. I could tell he was trying to decide if I was joking, being disrespectful, or if it was one of those new slang words that finally reached the Midwest.

The following guide will help you have a harmonious relationship with your parents.

How To Show Respect to Your Parents

Be Grateful – Say nice things to your parents whenever you have the chance. When your parents cook for you, let them know how much you loved it. You can also give them small gifts as a gesture of gratitude.

Take initiative - Do household chores without them asking. Let's face it, they're going to ask for help. You're going to eventually have to do the chores that are assigned to you. So, why not go ahead and do them without having to be asked or yelled at first. This reduces stress and strain on the relationship and your parents can appreciate that you consider yourself part of the team.

Don't Complain - Most of the time, parents ask you to do something to train you to do it when you're living on your own. Sometimes, as they grow older, they too need help, so don't complain. If you feel something is truly unfair, have a calm conversation about it and share your feelings and thoughts. It will be much more productive this way than whining, stomping off, slamming doors, or telling them how mean you think they are.

Understand their perspective - Look at it from your parent's perspective. Understand that your parents likely have to work a full time job, then they support each other and you and any siblings, and probably help out with the family pets as well, so they're probably tired. You get tired just having to run the vacuum or taking out the trash. Imagine having the responsibility for getting everything done. They need your help. They want your help. They deserve your help.

Follow Rules- Depending on who you listen to, there's an expression that says, 'Rules are made to be broken" and there is the primary mindset that rules are created for safety and protection. Your parents want the best for you. Sure, some rules may seem unfair, or made sense when you were younger, but you don't' think they should apply today. That's common. If that's your situation, have a calm conversation about how you feel. See if you can renegotiate the rules that no longer make sense.

Words Hurt - Be mindful of the words you're using. Sometimes the wrong words can create a reaction that you didn't intent, and even more often, one you didn't want. One of the big things children, even adult children, say that shatters your parent's hearts is that you hate them.

Logically, everyone knows it's not likely true, but it hurts. Try to ask yourself if something you're about to say would hurt you, if your parents said it to you instead. If so, think of a way to reword it. P.S. This applies to conversations with everyone, not just parents.

Body Language – The expressions on your face and the positioning of your arms and other ways you present yourself says what you're likely feeling. Sometimes a person can fake the body language, but if you're not paying attention, you may be sending hurtful signals.

Spend time - There was a day, long ago, when your parents thought, "Man, there's nothing I want more in this world than to have a little person. Someone I can love and take care of." Sure enough, there you were! Over the years, there has probably been great times and not-so-great times. That's normal.

One thing most parents didn't plan for was the time when you may not want to spend time with them anymore. You prefer hanging out with friends or just in your room alone. They probably miss spending time with you. They know you're growing up and becoming an adult as you age, but they still will miss the old days.

It's not the old you that they miss as they ooo-and-awe over your old photos, it's the memories of when you used to be joined at the hip and you hugged them and told them that you love them. You need to know; they don't miss the mini-you; they miss the you who used to show you loved them back.

Affection – Speaking of affection, don't wait until it's too late to tell your parents that you love them. A random hug and words of appreciation will do wonders to your relationship with them.

If you're not comfortable with hugging, try to start smaller, with casual smiles and a soft hand on their arm or some small step to inch your way into becoming comfortable with affection. It's not uncommon that people need to learn this vital show of affection. Take it one step at a time.

31

Humility - Don't talk back and know when to say you're sorry. Apologizing is another action that means the world to someone if they feel hurt by your actions. Again, take this a step at a time if you are uncomfortable with apologies.

You'll find it easiest if you say it quickly. If you stepped on someone's toe, you would quickly say, "Oh! Sorry." And that's acceptable. Follow a similar rule of thumb with your parents and those closest to you if you hurt them or their feelings.

Compromise – You may or may not have figured out that small arguments can ruin a relationship. Learn to compromise. This can prove that you're learning to adult like a pro. For example, let's say your bedtime is 9 PM, and you've had the same bedtime since you were eight. You're now fourteen and in high school.

A compromise could be you going to your parents and offering a compromise for a new bedtime. If you are allowed to stay up until 10 PM on weeknights, and midnight on weekends, you commit to not oversleeping in the mornings and making sure your weekend chores are done by noon on Saturdays.

This can also, in the world of adulting, be called 'making a case' which basically is you presenting an offer, asking for what you want, and telling the person who has authority on the decision, why it will help them (or at least not harm them) to be agreeable in your request.

There are some things you should never compromise on, like your integrity or knowing right from wrong, but much of adulting is about learning the art of compromise and finding a win/win situation when possible.

Don't lie or steal from them. This is the worst thing possible that would make your parents lose their trust in you. If ever you did this to them, promise yourself never to do it again.

Doing this, again and again, becomes a habit. This is a bad habit and will destroy your relationship— with friends as well as your parents. Once you break trust, it takes a long time to recover it. Try your best to avoid doing this to your parents.

Ask permission If you're going somewhere, or if you need to do or buy something, let your parents know first. Giving them a heads up and asking for permission is the best form of respect that parents want from their kids. Trust me, the expression 'It's better to beg forgiveness than ask permission," is flipped.

Don't cause worry – Let your parents know your whereabouts and the time when you're coming home. Some aren't given the authority to make these decisions. If you are, don't jeopardize the privilege and freedom.

The more you show respect for your parents, the less they're likely to grumble and complain.

Improving Your Relationship with Your Parents

Even if you become richer than Elon Musk, CEO of Tesla, you still cannot buy the most valuable things in this world.

The best things in life are those that money can't buy, and they have no perfect replacement. One example of that is TIME, and another is our family, particularly our parents.

We have limited time in this world. Your parents are also aging as you grow older.

Keep in mind that there will be less time together, especially if you're going to have a family of your own. So, while you're still living with your parents, make the most of it.

Our parents are not perfect, nor do they usually claim to be. You're still learning and growing, so it's important to realize that you don't know everything yet either. Since you both live in the same house, misunderstandings are bound to happen.

Have you experienced disrespecting your parents? Have you ever shouted at them or thrown a fit? Have you ever felt that time when you wish to be "free"? You find yourself wishing that you could live alone and away from your parents. Who hasn't?

But remember this, there would be a time in the future that you would wish to come back to, and that time would be NOW. Why? Because you still have your parents. You could still share memorable bonding moments with them.

You can say that you love them now. That's better than crying and wishing you could have said that while they were still around. That is the most common regret that most people have. Make sure you won't be one of them.

This is why even the wealthiest and most influential individuals in the world occasionally experience sadness or depression. Even if they buy anything they want, there is no replacement for our parents' love.

If you're not too close to your parents right now, there is still time to improve your relationship with them.

Spend Quality Time Together

Most people regret not spending time with their parents. They regret not being able to have more time together because all of you may be too busy with your separate lives.

One thing is certain in this world. We will all leave this world. You have to face the reality that someday, you are bound to lose one or both parents. Don't regret not having enough time with your parents. Start valuing them right now, while they're still around.

Spend quality time together. Building a stronger relationship isn't complicated. Start spending more time with your parents. Ask questions about them to get to know them more. Learn their quirks and favorite things and ask them about their experiences.

Find a hobby that you'd enjoy doing together. Your parents can be your friends too! Wouldn't it be nice if you had similar interests, hobbies, and passions?

If you don't, then find out what they like that you're interested in. You can build on that interest and, at the same time, have fun with your parents.

For example, if your dad likes fishing, you might ask him to teach you this important life skill. If your mom enjoys cooking, ask her to teach you her specialties which you can cook for your kids in the future.

Your parents may want to learn how to use console games too. They may even want to join you on your TikTok videos or online vlogs! Yes, some parents are cool like that! Some of them may want to share their favorite movies with you.

Helping them with the usual household chores makes these activities more enjoyable. It's a win-win situation! You'd get to share hard work so that not only will you be bonding with them, and you get to help them relax much earlier.

Most parents are working from home or doing hybrid work now after the COVID-19 pandemic. That means they have more time to spend with you. You can also ask your parents to teach you some life skills or life hacks that they like or use a lot.

Once you start doing things together, you'll look forward to more bonding time with them. Your parents would love that too. Most parents wish that their kids paid more time and attention to them. Spend quality time with your parents but don't treat it like it's an obligation. Do it because you love them, and you want to create more memories with them as they teach you more about life.

Trust me, making that bond that you share with your parents stronger is the best decision you'll ever make!

Communicate freely

Communicating with your parents is one way of understanding each other better. You'd get to have a closer bond if you knew more about each other. Be open to communicating your feelings, thoughts, and ideas.

Sometimes, we get so caught up with our lives that we forget that our parents are getting older. As the days go by, you feel more distant from each other because the communication is not there.

Improve your relationship with your parents by stepping up your communication skills. Get to know them better and talk about their interests as well as yours. Ask them about their younger days. Let them talk about how it was when they were the same age as you.

Talk about news, politics, relevant issues, etc. It would be more helpful if you talk about yourself. Talk to them about the problems that are bothering you, what you're anxious about, or a project you'd like to work on. Ask them about their day and what they feel about their work and the workplace. The more you share thoughts and opinions with each other, the closer you'll get.

Include parents in your life

Your parents are always looking out for your best interests. They have looked after you since you were born and have guided you as much as they can. They're involved with your growing up even before you are born. You are their light and one of the reasons why they're working so hard. The least you can do is to include them in your life plans, family events, trips, and vacations.

Offer and Ask for Advice

Remember the time when you were a kid, and you fell, scraped your knee, or broke something, and you ended up crying? Who was there to pick you up and comfort you?

That's right! It's either your mom or dad or both. If you feel that they're overstepping your boundaries, step back and think. Are you being too sensitive? Your parents desire the best for you. Give them a chance to share their thoughts and advice. They're coming from a different perspective from you, and that's a good thing.

Your parents are there to guide you and give you sound advice. Don't hesitate to ask for their opinions and advice. They understand you well and unlike some people, they will not judge you nor look down on you. All you need to do is open up to them.

They'd always give you their advice and look out for you. If you see your parents struggling with something, return the favor and offer to help them too. They might need your advice about what gadgets to buy, what restaurants or food they should try, etc.

Disagree in a Respectful Manner

Disagreements are part of any relationship. It doesn't feel good, but we all have our opinions and differences. What's important is that there is still respect for each other. Even if your parents don't see it "your way," respect that they are still an authority in your life. You still live under their wings, so you need to follow their rules.

Choice of words and tone of voice is very important when disagreeing with your parents. Instead of saying "you're wrong", say "I disagree because." That makes a big difference. With the first one, you're already saying that you think they're wrong. While in the second statement, you're stating that you have a different opinion. No matter how upset you are, control the volume of your voice and don't yell at them.

Though it's hard to disagree with your parents, you still have the right to voice your opinion. But do it in a respectful manner. They may be having a disagreement with you, but it may be because they're concerned about you. Remember that parents always have your best interest in mind.

Give Them Gifts

People love gifts! Who doesn't? Receiving gifts is the best part of a special occasion, whether it's Christmas or Birthdays.

Parents always make sure that they give us the best gifts possible even if there's no occasion. They plan and look out for signs on what to get. They'd even ask friends or look at the latest gadgets, gaming consoles, clothing, etc.

If you think about it, you likely realize that you're usually on the receiving end. It's time to show your appreciation and love for your parents by giving them a gift too. It doesn't need to be a holiday, birthday, or Mother's/Father's Day.

Gifts come in all kinds of forms. You can give them something that they need. You can also ask them or see what they want to buy but can't. That's because they're always thinking of your needs as the top priority. You can also give them something that they don't see the need to replace until it's dilapidated, like a wallet or a bag. It doesn't even need to involve money. You can make something by hand or use your creative skills. You can cook for them or fix something that they haven't got the time to get fixed. Doing deep cleaning of the house or helping them do their chores is already a big thing for them.

It shows how much you care and love them. Your parents will definitely appreciate your thoughtfulness. Gifting them something is even more fun than receiving gifts from them. You'll feel good inside, especially when they appreciate your gifts.

Want to really show them love? Write them a sincere letter (bonus points if you write it by hand), telling them something that they did for you, that you appreciate.

Long after they're gone, you will likely find all your gratitude letters stored away for safekeeping and to reflect on when they are feeling sad, depressed, or like they're failing at parenting. Don't expect a major reaction from them, though. Some parents have a habit of keeping their emotions intact. Even if they look like they didn't appreciate it, they're celebrating inside.

Try to keep in mind that your parents were once in the same positions you are in. They were babies, kids, teens, and young adults, and whether they had a better or worse childhood than you, they faced a time when they had to try to understand that the rulebook for kids is different than the rulebook for adults. Just like you, they had to learn to see things differently and had to recognize that their parents may have been trying to help them see more, understand more, and make better decisions.

To this day, no matter how confident your parents may seem in front of you, it's important to understand that they probably feel like they're not doing as good of a job as they should. Their love for you is there, no matter how they show it.

Though there may be times when you don't see eye to eye, and you won't be on a BFF level with your parents. It's beneficial to have a good relationship with them. You'll always have someone to confide in. You'll have someone to support you, push you to achieve more in life, yet accept you for who you are.

HOUSEKEEPING
MAINTENANCE & COOKING

CHAPTER 1

H: HOUSEKEEPING, MAINTENANCE, & COOKING

The skills and information found in this chapter are normally taught by your parents, but you can also do self-learning and apply these at home, so you have some practice before you decide to have your own family or move out in the future.

Let's face it, you may feel like your parents view you as an obligation more than a treasure. I get it. I felt that way at times too, when I was younger, but as a parent, I realize how tough it can be, especially as a single parent, to keep the bills paid, and the roof over our heads, and wonder if anyone even sees how hard it is to pull it all together.

Aside from ensuring that I earn enough to provide for my family's needs, to have enough to pay for tuition fees, bills, and other expenses, it's very difficult to maintain the house too. Your help with the household chores, maintenance, and occasional cooking will help you display your love and appreciation for your parents in a big way.

You are not an obligation to your parent(s). They may be struggling in order to keep up with all of their obligations, but it is up to you to help ease the pressure off of them. Your help will not only help them physically but will also energize and motivate them to keep going.

Think of your family as a team in a relay race. You need to help run the race by taking the baton of responsibility from their hands by helping around the house. That is a huge burden off their shoulders. They can concentrate on their other tasks as you get more tasks done and your family can cross the finish line together. They'll have more time to relax and enjoy time with you and the rest of the family and your relationship will be stronger.

Housekeeping

Making Your Bed

Your bed is where you spend one-third of your life. It's a place that gives you comfort and makes you feel good and relaxed. It only takes a few minutes to make it look great after you wake up.

Here's what you can do to make your bed:
1. Remove things on top because you'll need to lift the covers.
2. Remove the covers and shake off some of the dirt and dust. You can also vacuum the mattress first before you lay down and secure the covers.
3. Secure and smooth out the covers so that they stay in place. You need to know the types of bed covers, what their functions are, and the arrangement of the bed covers.
4. Tuck the covers in to keep them in place.
5. After the covers are secure, plump and place the pillows and quilt or throw on top of the bed.

Easy right? You still need to know the different bed covers, toppers, and bed protectors to make this skill a success. Some of the covers are optional.

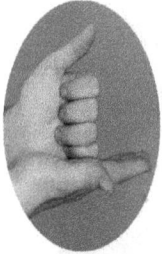

REMINDERS FOR PEOPLE WITH INJURY OR DISABILITY

Making your bed is fairly easy to do on your own, especially when you practice this often. If you haven't done this before, have someone assist you so you can remember how to position yourself next time when you do it on your own.

If vacuuming will not be done, all the tasks can be done independently. However, assistance may be needed if you're going to lift and relocate heavy mattresses and bed covers.

This is so you can do the vacuuming with ease. Remember that a little assistance is better than having to deal with possible injury.

Bed Sheets & Protectors

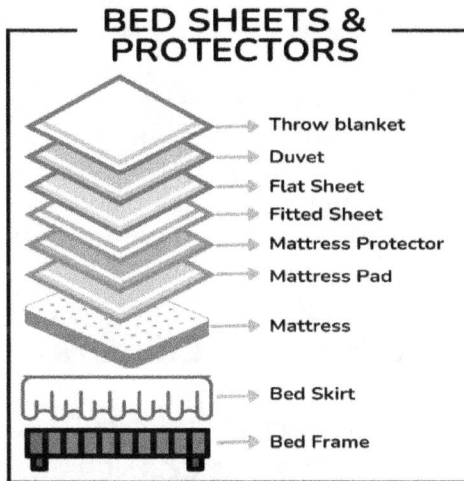

BED SHEETS & PROTECTORS

- Throw blanket
- Duvet
- Flat Sheet
- Fitted Sheet
- Mattress Protector
- Mattress Pad
- Mattress
- Bed Skirt
- Bed Frame

Dust ruffle or bed skirt

This is applied before the actual mattress. Bed skirts should be long enough to almost touch the floor but short enough not to rest on the floor.

Mattress pad

A mattress pad is an optional layer that you can add to make the mattress more comfortable. It has different textures and firmness.

Mattress protector

Your mattress's lifespan is increased by using a mattress protector. It is like a fitted sheet that goes around your entire mattress.

It protects the mattress from spills, stains, night sweats, etc. It serves as a barrier between you and the allergens found on your bed. Dust mites, pet dander, and mildew might be in your mattress.

It comes in waterproof fabric like Polyurethane. It

49

stops any liquid from penetrating the cover but still allows airflow. Inexpensive options include plastic and vinyl.

It should have good material. Usually, the flat sheet and the fitted sheet come together and are bought as a set. Buy flat sheets that have thread counts between 200-800, depending on your budget. You can secure the flat sheet to your bed using the hospital fold or hospital corners.

How to Do Hospital Corners

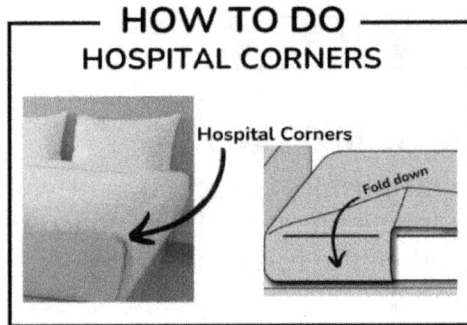

Hospital corners are the most popular type of fold intended for flat sheets to make your bed look neat. Imagine your flat sheet is a gift wrapper. Remember how you fold the sides to make a triangle before you fold it down to tape it?

That's what you need to do at the ends of the flat sheet. First, fold one end of the flat sheet where it is hanging loose. Lift and create a 45-degree angle at the corner of the mattress then fold it downwards. Tuck the excess part of the flat sheet as neatly as possible. Do this for all remaining corners.

Duvet or Comforter

Comforters are the fluffiest layer of your bed. It gives you warmth and makes your bed more comfortable to be in. Usually, comforter fillers are synthetic down, but some are from cotton, wool, or silk.

Duvets and Duvet Covers are a cross between the comforter and the fitted sheet. Duvet inserts are like comforters but tacked inside a duvet cover.

They are more preferred than Comforters because they're easier to remove. The downside is that they're difficult to put on the bed.

Throw Blankets and Quilts

These are optional. Throw blankets are usually used when it's too hot and uncomfortable inside the duvet.

NOTE: You can use as many pillows as you like if there is enough space for them.

Importance of changing/cleaning sheets

Washing your sheets and using clean sheets can boost your happiness level. It can make you feel more relaxed because it boosts your mood and de-stresses you. What happens when you don't change your sheets often?

You're exposing yourself to dust mites, bacteria, fungi, animal fur, etc. Other things found on sheets include sweat, dead skin cells, and other body excrements.

This leads to skin irritation, allergies, and skin problems. Dirty sheets also activate your sinusitis and asthma.

How often should you wash your bedding?

- Wash all bed sheets, blankets, pillowcases, and duvet covers 1-2 times a week, depending on the season and your body sweat. If you sweat heavily, wash it at least twice a week. If not, a weekly wash schedule is alright.
- Wash the comforters, based on need, monthly or quarterly (four times a year, with each new season). If it contains special and sensitive fillers, have it dry-cleaned at least twice a year.
- Wash mattress covers monthly.
- Wash Bed Skirts twice a year.

What's important is that you make your bed every morning. In only takes a couple of minutes to make a good and beneficial habit. Imagine how nice it feels to go to bed with a well-made and crisp-looking bed.

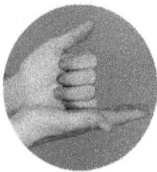

REMINDERS FOR PEOPLE WITH INJURY OR DISABILITY

Cleaning & Setting Up Your Room

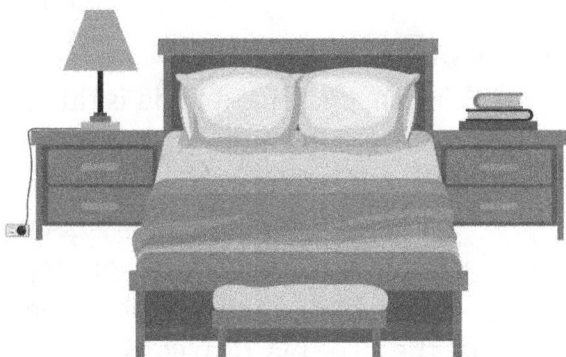

It's your room so it's your responsibility to keep it clean and safe.

Having a dirty room may affect your overall well-being and it also affects your mental health because it's harder to think when you're not comfortable in your room.

This is probably the simplest of all household chores and it's a responsibility that only you should do to keep your privacy.

To help you clean your room, you should have lightweight mops and vacuums so it's easier to carry and use. Request help if you feel the need to move heavy objects.

Wear protective masks if you have an allergy to dust.

Cleaning Your Room

Remove all clutter
The very first thing that you need to do is throw away all the garbage. Remove all clutter from your bed and desktop.

Either place them in a single section of your room or use a box or large plastic bag to put all the random things inside. Note that the large plastic bag should be separate from those that you consider garbage. Use different colors of plastic bags or containers to avoid confusion.

Don't forget to check under your bed and any hidden areas. If you have old food, throw them in the garbage bag.

Place all the dirty plates, cups, spoons, and other utensils in the kitchen for cleaning. Clean these items immediately to avoid pests.

Organize all pieces of clothing lying around
Pick up all your clothes and socks and determine if they are clean or dirty. If they are clean, fold or hang them and place them inside your dresser and closet.

If they are dirty, place them in the laundry basket. As a rule of thumb, treat them like they're dirty unless you're sure that they're clean.

Don't wash them immediately. You might find another article of clothing while cleaning your room.

Wash the bed sheets and pillowcases

Remove the bed sheets and pillowcases and place them in a hamper. Do not combine these with your clothes nor wash them together.

Also, look out for plush toys and similar items that need washing. If curtains are also dirty, remove and wash the curtains and replace them with clean ones. You can put these batches in the laundry while you're cleaning your room.

Remove Dust and Dirt

Use a vacuum, duster, and broom to rid your room of dust and dirt. Find a scrap of cloth or an old piece of clothing that you no longer use.

Dampen it and use it to wipe cabinets, wardrobes, windows, and tables. Make sure that you wring it well so that it's only a little damp and not too wet.

Mop or sweep the floor. Do the mopping and sweeping at least once a week.

Don't be a pack rat

Donate good-quality items that you no longer need but are still useful for others. Throw away broken items that are irreparable. if still fixable, set it aside in a corner for fixing later.

Recycle the paper and cardboard that holds no sentimental value. Donate books, clothes, and toys that you no longer need to create more space for you in your room.

Organize your items

Move back the items to their original location and assigned places. It would help if you had a box or container to help organize your room.

You can buy organizer boxes in supermarkets as well as craft stores if you have many pens and papers. Buy the boxes AFTER you've cleaned your room.

That way, you know exactly what size of boxes or containers you need. Make sure these boxes have a specific spot in your room. Label the boxes before placing them somewhere accessible.

Less is more

Display near your study/worktable some frames and designs. You can also display plush toys or figures, or anything that will make you happy when you look at it. This will help you feel good and make you concentrate more.

Disinfect items and fixtures

Spray household disinfectant spray on the door handles, tables, and fixtures. Be careful when handling switches as you might get shocked.

Wipe Your Windows and Mirrors

Use glass cleaners and microfiber cloth to clean glasses, windows, and mirrors. Use a crumpled newspaper to wipe down windows.

Vacuum and clean window tracks. You can use an old toothbrush to sweep off the dirt that is sticking too much and your vacuum cannot reach or clean.

Create a checklist
Write down all of the things you need to do and clean so that you won't miss anything. You can set the priority on tasks to do based on the list.

Play happy and energetic music
Play some music to inspire you and get you going. It should have a happy and inspirational vibe. This will help you be energized as you work through your to-do list. Many have said they get into the zone and don't even recall it feeling like chores at all. Music can heal many dilemmas!

Cleaning The Kitchen

Cleaning the kitchen is very important to avoid the buildup of grease and to avoid pests from settling in your kitchen area. Your health may be compromised if these pests decide to stay because of a poorly cleaned kitchen area.

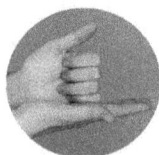

REMINDERS FOR PEOPLE WITH INJURY OR DISABILITY

While cleaning the kitchen is easy, some tasks such as unclogging the kitchen sink, or the garbage disposal system may require some assistance. If you think that the situation requires professional help, don't hesitate to get it to avoid further damage to the tools and fixtures.

Spray Cleaners

You can make your own spray cleaners using the most basic items as seen below. Please ensure that both kids and pets are not exposed to the solution inside the spray cleaners.

HOW TO MAKE YOUR OWN
SPRAY CLEANERS

All Purpose Cleaner

2 tsp. Baking Soda
1 tsp. Dish Soap
4 Tbsp. White Vinegar
1 3/4 cup Warm Water
Stir to mix.
Transfer to Spray Bottle.

Glass Cleaner

1/4 Rubbing Alcohol
1/4 cup White Vinegar
1 Tbps Corn Starch
2 Cups Warm Water
Stir to mix.
Transfer to Spray Bottle.

Dusting Spray

2 tsp Olive Oil
1 tsp. Lemon Juice
1/4 cup White Vinegar
1 cup Warm Water
Transfer to Spray Bottle.

Toilet Bowl Cleaner

1/4 cup Baking Soda
1/4 cup Borax
1 cup White Vinegar
Mix gently.
Apply to Toilet Bowl.
Leave for 30 minutes.
Use a bowl brush to scrub.

Grout Cleaner

1/2 cup Baking Soda
1/4 cup Rubbing Alcohol
1/4 cup White Vinegar
Mix gently.
Apply solution using an old toothbrush.
Leave for 5 minutes.
Rinse.

Sink

To clean the sink, wipe the basin to avoid mold growth and water stains. The water stains will wipe off using a sponge dipped in warm soapy water. Make sure that you also wash and rinse the fixtures of the sink.

Another way of cleaning the sink of stubborn water stains is to mix baking soda and white vinegar using a 1:2 ratio. Sprinkle the baking soda on the sink, especially parts with stubborn stains.

Pour white vinegar and allow it to fizzle for about 10-15 minutes before wiping the mixture off. You can also use a store bought all-purpose cleaner.

Faucet

Use an old toothbrush to clean the corners and hard-to-reach areas of the faucet. You can also use baking soda and vinegar to remove the water spots. Buff it off once you're done so that the faucet remains shiny.

Cabinets and Counters

Check the items inside for expired items. Throw away items that seem spoiled. Use the vacuum cleaner to remove dust and crumbs. Wipe the inside of the cabinets with a wet piece of rag then wipe them using a dry rag. Wooden cabinets have specific cleaning supplies and sprays made for wood.

Since wood has a tendency of reacting easily to chemicals and liquids, it is very important to pick the sprays and cleaners that are made specifically for wood to avoid damage from watermarks, mold, or rot.

Note: Unless you're on your own, always check with the person who bought the expired foods or broken items before you throw anything away. It shows them respect and allows them to make a final decision on what should be thrown out or donated.

Kitchen Counters

Wipe the counters using a sponge and water with soap. Wipe until everything is dry using a clean cloth. You may use antibacterial sprays or wipes to clean the counters after you're done cooking. If your counter is granite or stone, make sure to use the correct type of cleaning supplies made for that item.

Stovetop

Wipe the burners using a damp rag. Some electric burners are removable and washed with warm water and soap.

Some are even washable using a dishwasher. If your burners are electric, use a damp rag or sponge to wipe them.

Stove Surface

Use a sponge and soap to wipe the stove surface. If you have the budget, buy Clorox wipes, which remove stains and grease better.

Vent Hood

Use the damp rag with soap to clean the vent hood. A damp cloth can remove the suds. Make sure to use a dry cloth afterward. Clean the vent filters once a month by soaking them in warm and soapy water.

Oven

Remove and soak the grates in warm, soapy water for hours until it's easier to remove the dirt. Use a scouring pad to scrub the grates afterward.

Fridge

Remove all the food from your fridge and check the items if they are already expired. Separate the fresh ones from the expired food. Throw away food items that have gone bad and take note of which ones they are. You can buy a replacement for them once you go grocery shopping again.

Make a cleaning solution for the inner part of the fridge. Combine 2 tablespoons of baking soda with 1 small glass of water. Using a damp sponge dipped into the cleaning solution, wipe down the inner part of the fridge. Use another wet rag to wipe the inner shelves and sides, then use a clean rag to dry everything. Scrub out the stains and sticky items. Make sure not to forget to clean the drawers and shelves.

Repeat the same process in the built-in freezer. You will likely want to use clean warm water to counteract the colder surfaces.

Freezer

You may have a separate freezer. If so, it may have a buildup of ice inside. This will require a manual defrost and cleaning process. To do this, first unplug the freezer and remove all the frozen items. Place rags around the refrigerator door. If your refrigerator is not frost free, you need to wait until the freezer defrosts.

While defrosting, create the cleaning solution. Combine 1 cup of water, 1 teaspoon of dish soap, and 1 teaspoon of white vinegar. If you have an extra spray bottle, you can use this to spray the solution in the freezer. If you don't have a spray bottle, use a damp sponge or rag. Wipe it inside the freezer. Afterward, wipe everything with clean paper towels and dry it well.

Once everything is dry, move back all the frozen. Move all refrigerated items into their respective places.

NOTE: Modern appliances have a stainless steel covering. While this is an appealing look, there may be special cloths or cleaners that will allow you to wipe the exteriors without causing streaking. Read your manuals to see if they suggest anything specific.

Additionally, there are various types of countertops across the world. Same as with appliances, make sure to check if there are special suggestions for how to clean these special materials.

Floor

Use the broom to sweep the kitchen area from dust, crumbs, and other garbage. Mop the floor when necessary. Do this at least once every week so that it would be easier to clean the floor next time. Once you are done, put back all the cleaning tools to their right place. Remember, "A place for everything, and everything in its place"

Trash

Once you're done doing the cleaning, it's now time to take out the trash. Do this last because while you're cleaning, you'll keep finding things that need to be tossed. Make sure the trash can is clean too. Wash it well and allow it to air dry.

Garbage Disposal

Why is it clogged?
Have you noticed that your kitchen sink is having a hard time draining? Most of the time it is because there are objects that block it. First, to troubleshoot, you want to look, don't touch. If you have two sinks, one may have a garbage disposal that can be very dangerous if you're not careful.

A garbage disposal pulverizes all the food waste that your family puts into the sink to small bits of food that will easily wash down the drain. This is usually the side that causes the clogging.

The other side often has a barrier that only allows water and very small bits of food through, so you will be able to easily remove any larger pieces and throw them in the trash.

The disposal side though, looks like a rubber barrier with a small opening. On the other side of that rubber opening is likely the problem... but also the contraption that can shred food products from full sized to tiny pieces of unrecognizable food.

You should never put your hand into this hole unless you are absolutely certain you have a full understanding of where the power switch is, you have power disconnected, and even then, only if you have someone with you, to provide immediate assistance if something goes wrong.

Lack of water flow
When you're not using enough water to dispose of the food waste, this can lead to a slow buildup. After some time, the buildup will clog the disposal drain. Try flushing the sink with water.

Grinding items that cause clogs
There are some items that contribute to clogging the disposal drain faster. Examples of these are Coffee grounds, banana peels, potato peels, and eggshells. Fruit and vegetable peels form a thick paste that accumulates and stops the drain from doing its job.

Stuck Foreign Objects
Foreign objects include toys, silverware, and anything that isn't food or biodegradable. Also included are the inorganic wastes such as tin foil, paper, and plastic.

Liquid fat, Oil & Grease
Believe it or not, even liquid items such as liquid fat, oil, and grease can result in a clogged drain too. Always use the hottest water possible to wash these down.

Food Scraps

- Choose the proper container for your needs. Repurpose an old coffee or yogurt container or buy something new with a tight lid to keep odors at bay.
- Choose a location for your container to be stored.
- If you're not sure whether to use a plastic or compostable bag, check with your local recycling program.
- To keep your outdoor trash dumpster pest-free and cleaner, keep food scraps in the fridge or freezer until collection day.

Steps to Unclog the Kitchen's Garbage Disposal

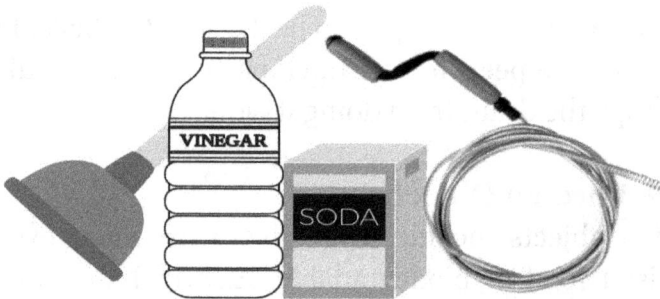

Step 1: Shut Off the Power Switch & Unplug the Garbage Disposal System

For most Garbage disposal systems, the switch is under the cabinet. Some of the switches are on walls nearby.

If it's impossible to find the switch, turn off the breaker from the main power panel. This is to ensure that you won't get electrocuted. This would also ensure that it won't turn on on its own due to a defective switch.

Step 2: Check the Garbage Disposal for clogs using a flashlight.

Using a flashlight, light up the disposal and check if you can see what seems to be causing the blockage. If it is something you can see using this means, use long nose pliers to grab the item and dispose of it.

Step 3: Use a Natural Cleaner

Don't immediately turn to chemical cleaners. Use a natural cleaner to break up the clog caused by food waste. To create this natural cleanser, mix 1/2 cup of vinegar with 1/4 cup of baking soda.

Make sure to mix the solution before you pour it into the drain. After pouring, wait for 10-20 minutes. Before the 20 minutes is over, boil a liter of water and while it's piping hot, pour it down the drain. This should unclog the food waste.

If it doesn't work, go to Step 4.

Step 4: Plunge the Drain

If the natural cleaner didn't work, it's now time to use a kitchen plunger. Kitchen plungers should be different from the ones used for your toilet.

If you have no choice but to use the toilet plunger for this, use it. Ensure that you clean and sanitize everything including the sink. Before you plunge the drain, clamp off the dishwasher connection hose if it's present.

This will help prevent the dirty water from flowing back into the dishwasher itself. It helps stop making a mess of your dishwasher.

Once you're done clamping the hose, put the plunger over the drain. Then pour some water into your sink and make sure that the water is covering the tip of the plunger.

Once the water begins to flow, begin plunging the drain. If it flows, the disposal has been cleared of clog. More hot water should be poured down the drain to clear any blockage.

Step 5: Turn the Disposal Blades & Pick Out Debris

You may need to rotate the blades using your hands to reach the debris. That's why it's very important to follow Step 1.

You don't want to lose a finger! So, it's very important to turn off the power. As you turn the disposal blades, you are breaking the clog so you can grab it from the blades.

Step 6: Clean the P-Trap or S-Trap

If plunging fails and turning the disposal blades won't unclog the drain, then look at the pipes. Garbage disposal units are usually attached to either the P-Trap or the S-Trap. These traps look like this:

Remove the trap using pliers and clean the pipes well. Since the shapes of these traps are not straight, debris can accumulate and block the drain.

Don't forget to use a catch basin or a bucket to catch the liquid and debris. Use the pliers to loosen the slip-nut fittings on the trap, so it's easier to remove them.

If dissembling of all parts is not possible, use a drain snake or a coat hanger to remove the blockages. Do not use chemicals to dislodge the blockages. Because chemicals can destroy the plastic parts of the kitchen garbage disposal.

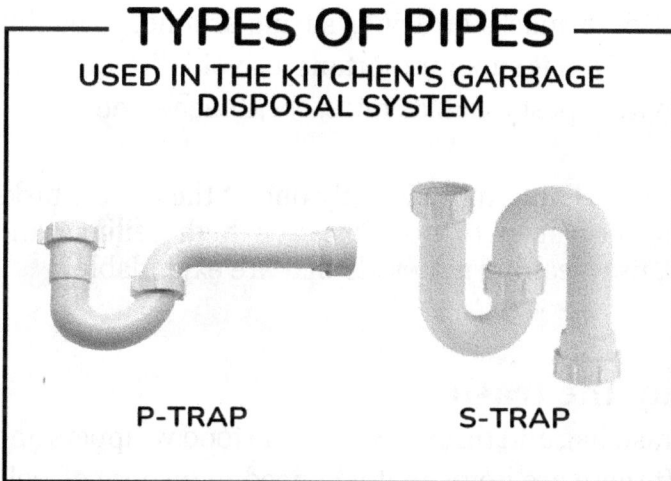

TYPES OF PIPES
USED IN THE KITCHEN'S GARBAGE DISPOSAL SYSTEM

P-TRAP   S-TRAP

Cleaning The Living Room

Your living room is where you can relax and spend time with the family, so it's important to make sure you don't leave leftover snacks or drinks sitting around. Cleaning the living room is super important to avoid dirt and trash from inviting pests such as mice, cockroaches, etc.

Cleaning the living room is truly one of the easiest tasks you may be asked to do. To reach high ceilings and shelves, use cleaning materials that are extendable.

Pick up the trash

Use a trash bag and throw away all the food wrappers and trash. If there are items that you need to dispose of, sell, or donate, separate them. Now is the time to get rid of unwanted items or those that you wouldn't use anymore.

Declutter and reorganize

Remove the clutter that's out of place and place them back where it should be. If possible, create or buy storage for toys, video games, books, papers, mail, etc. This way, there's a place for everything. This may be a great time to buy that new game case you've been checking out! Maybe suggest a keyholder for your parents as well. They'll appreciate you looking out for them.

Straighten up the sofa

Fluff the pillows, remove the dust, and straighten the seat cushions. Use a vacuum to pick up food particles, breadcrumbs, dust, hair, fur, or lint on the sofa. Don't hesitate to pull out the cushions and dig into the sofa. I've found money in the living room furniture more times than I can count! Finders Keepers in this case!

Dust the Surfaces

Use a clean microfiber cloth to get rid of the dust from the surfaces of the TV, coffee table, and shelves. A feather duster is also useful to remove dust. Organize the area for cleaning, starting from the very top to the bottom. This way, when dust falls, you don't have to clean some areas twice. Trust me on this one. I've learned the hard way!

Organize the Coffee Table and Magazine Rack

If you still have a magazine rack, remove magazines that are too old or worn out. Wipe the books and magazines as well. Unless your family has a favorite issue that they like to reread, it's best to toss or donate older issues.

If you have books sitting around, make sure they find their way back to the right shelf or display area. It's easy to set them down and forget them. Books hold dreams, secrets, and vital tips that deserve to be protected.

Vacuum or Shake out Rugs

Tidy up the positions of the carpets and throw rugs. Vacuum the carpet at least weekly. If you have a pet, then that may need to be done even more often.

Clean the Ceiling Fan and Light Fixtures

Remove cobwebs and dust from the ceiling fan and light fixtures. Extendable dusters are available that make this very simple. Watch your eyes if you're working overhead.

Vacuum the Blinds and Curtains

Wash the curtains, as needed, to remove dust. Many do it more often, but at least once a year during "Spring Cleaning" time should be the minimum. Vacuum the blinds as well. If you have quality blinds, these should be cleaned often.

If you have the type that would be considered disposable, many people will rather replace them than wash them as it's not an easy task. That said, if you do it regularly, you can maintain anything longer than if you ignore it until it's too late.

The Floors

As you move around removing dust from other locations, most of the dust will accumulate on the floor. It depends on what the flooring type is. If carpet, vacuum. If tile, wood, or vinyl, sweep and mop. You may be tempted to vacuum a bare floor. Unless it's a vacuum specifically intended for bare flooring, you may find you'll make more of a mess than it's worth. Grab a broom or steam mop and be done with it.

You may want to try to a vacuum robot. They help keep the floors clean without your effort. It can be a fun gadget, but it's another item to maintain and not yet cost efficient for most.

Polish Furniture

You can buy a wood furniture polish or simply use a dust cloth. Over time, wood benefits from occasional treatment to keep it from drying out or aging too quickly. Investigate what your furniture is made of. Is it solid wood or is it laminated? If laminated, a damp cloth may be all you need.

One tip, if you use an oil based polish, make sure you rub it in completely as leaving residue on your wooden furniture can cause damage to the wood. Always read the container's instructions.

Windows and Mirrors

Wash the windows as needed. This is another great Spring Cleaning item to keep on your checklist. You may need to clean them more often, especially if you have pets or young people around.

As for the mirrors, it's a good idea to clean these at least weekly (especially in the bathrooms). Use a glass cleaner and spray lightly over full mirror. Rub paper towel all around, making sure to clear gunk from brushing your teeth. Then, with a new cloth, wipe completely dry, to avoid streaking. Scrub down horizontally. Use microfiber to clean and remove fingerprints and residue.

Cleaning The Bathroom

Cleaning the bathroom regularly helps avoid buildup of mildew and lime. It also makes the bathroom more comfortable, relaxing, and hygienic to use.

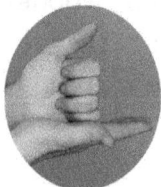

REMINDERS FOR PEOPLE WITH INJURY OR DISABILITY

Use a grabber tool in case you need to clean hard to reach areas. If you're using a wheelchair, try to transfer to a low-rise stool or chair that would enable you to clean more steadily.

Gather Trash

First, empty trash cans and replace the plastic bag inside if you use liners. Liners make it super easy to avoid future cleanings of the gunk that ends up in the bottom of trash cans, but if you're trying to avoid landfill material, cleaning is a green choice.

Clear Vanity Items from the Countertop

Move the makeup, razors, toothbrush, and toothpaste before you start cleaning. This keeps dirt away from them and makes it less of a hassle to keep moving them while cleaning.

You may be tempted to just wipe around these things, but don't trick yourself into thinking you're saving time by wiping around things. When it's done, it will be evident that there's dust around the items that you didn't pick up. If your parents come by for a *quality control check*, expect to be called out on this one! It's surprising how pleased you'll be with yourself knowing you've done a great job with this task, and even better, once your parent comments on how great you did (or at least didn't comment on what a bad job it was).

Use a Bathroom Cleanser

Use a bathroom cleanser to clean the bathroom areas. Apply it to the shower area, countertops, bathtub, and sink. Choose a cleanser that helps remove mildew and soap scum.

Use a stronger cleanser specially made for toilets when you clean the toilet. Also, it's a good idea to use some sort of gloves or a tool with a handle/wand so you don't have to touch the chemicals or bacteria that grows in the toilet. That said, many people use a washcloth and swish their hands around in the bowl to clean it. If you choose to do that, keep it brief and wash your hands afterward.

Caution: You should always make sure that the bathroom is well ventilated. Wear the right type of gloves and face mask. This is to avoid inhaling the fumes. These will also help you avoid the strong chemicals from damaging your hands.

Clean the Toilet

Squirt a strong bleach or toilet cleaner inside the toilet bowl, including the inside rim. It is preferable to use a toilet cleaner especially made for this. Some may be tempted to clean only the inside of the bowl, but there are many parts of a toilet that need to be cleared of grime and germs. Clean the flush handle and the area around the seat using a damp rag and cleanser or a leave-on antibacterial spray.

Clean Tub, Shower, and Grout

If the cleaner used doesn't remove the bathroom grime on the tiles, here are some other ways to remove them:

As you clean the tub/shower area, there is likely tile or a fiberglass surround. Whatever it is, make sure you use the cleanser that is labeled all-purpose or specifically targeted to the material you have.

It really will depend on what cleaner you use, so as always, read the label of the product you're going to use. The directions on the manufacturer's label should supersede all other suggestions and tips.

It's easy to skip the tile if you've cleaned the tub and fixtures, but if you skip the tile too many times, you'll start to see the grout turning colors. Sometimes it may be reddish pink, others dark colored, even a greenish blue. While I love colors as much as the next person...these colors are not your friend! Alert an adult and they can help you get the areas clean. These moldy or bacteria-filled areas should be approached cautiously. If you are the adult, protect yourself from skin contact and clean fully.

Vacuum or Wash the Bathmats or Carpets.

Bathmats are just like your bath towels. They should be washed. Depending on what type you have, there may be a coating on the bottom to keep it from slipping. They should all be machine washable, but you may want to read the care label to verify if it can be put in a dryer.

While you want to wash your bath towels at least once a week (many people prefer more often), your floor mats can probably go once a month. If someone is potty training or otherwise missing the toilet bowl when they use the restroom, you may want to ensure they're washed more often. The smell of stale urine in a small area can be downright gross!

Mop the Bathroom Floor

Use a mop or damp rag to pick up the dirt, dust, and debris from the bathroom floor. Depending on the size of your bathroom, you may find it simpler to get a washcloth wet with floor cleaner and simply run across the floor, making sure to get around the toilet, behind the trash can, etc. You'd be surprised how much hair falls to the floor. You probably don't even see it, but hair product residue from spray bottles and other overspray are also building up on the floor. It should be done at least weekly but depending on the level of use and how messy the occupants are, this could probably be a monthly task.

Vacuuming the House

TIP#1: One way to avoid dust and dirt in the house is to keep a shoe rack at your home's entrance. This way, you don't have to spread the dirt inside the house and your room. You can place bedroom slippers near the entrance, which you can wear when you're inside the house. Don't have a shoe rack? Drop your shoes at the door anyway.

Vacuuming the house is a simple but tedious task. This is because you must go over and over the same area. Not all the dust, hair, and fur get captured during a single run, so you have to go over the same area to ensure it's clean. Many vacuums now have a light sensor to help you know if it's stopped picking up debris. Otherwise, listen for the debris to stop sounding as it's sucked up.

How many times do you vacuum in a month?

Vacuuming weekly is ideal. Some vacuum daily because they like to have the freshly swept pattern a vacuum often makes. Others may have pets or little people, both making daily vacuuming logical. Make it a routine habit or schedule so you don't forget.

How do vacuum hard-to-reach areas?

Some areas are more difficult to vacuum. That's why you need to use the other attachments of your vacuum cleaner. These parts help clean hard-to-reach areas better.

How to vacuum allergens and small dust particles?

HEPA means High-Efficiency Particulate Air. These types of vacuums are capable of filtering and trapping small types of particles in the air.

HEPA vacuums filter your house and room and freshen it up in a few minutes. Leave it running for longer and your room will smell and feel cleaner. This is best for those who have an allergy to pollen, dust, and other air particles, as well as those who have asthma.

SAFETY PRECAUTION NEEDED!

SAFETY FIRST

- Always practice safety precautions.
- Do not proceed if you might hurt yourself.
- Request supervision & help if needed.
- Check or test for allergic reactions prior to using any chemicals or ingesting food items.
- If you are injured, too young for the task, or if you have disabilities, you may experience some difficulties doing some specific tasks. Please ask for assistance and guidance when doing the tasks to ensure your overall safety.

Mopping The Floors

TIP#1: Check what cleaning product you need for your floor as some floors are wood, marble tiles, and so on. Buy the correct cleaning product.

Choose a Mop and Bucket that suits the types of floors you have as well. For example, if your floor has a lot of texture such as ceramic tiles, buy a strip mop. If you have a smooth floor, use a sponge mop. Buy mop buckets with built-in wringers that can accommodate the size of your mop.

Here's some tips on how to mop the floors:

• Clear the floor space as much as you can. Lift chairs and tables, as well as small furniture, coffee table, side table, rugs, and carpets.

• Sweep the area first using a broom. Use the vacuum to clear small dust particles, crumbs, and dirt to make mopping more efficient.

- A bucket should be filled with WARM water and the appropriate amount of floor-cleaning fluid. Note that this depends on what type and color of flooring you have.

- Soak the mop into the bucket of water and cleaning solution. Turn the mop around the bucket to ensure that the cleaning product is well mixed into the warm water.

- Lift the mop and remove excess water. Some mops have automatic levers. Others such as the sponge type have a lever that you need to press to squeeze out excess water.

- Some mops buckets have a wringer which you use to remove the excess water. We only need a damp mop and not one that drips as you move it around. If it's dripping, wring it out more.

- Always start from the corner of the room farthest from the door and do it in small sections. This will make each stroke of the mop more effective.

- Change the water and cleaning solution if it becomes too murky.

- Advise the people living with you that you're mopping a specific area. So that they stay off the floor until it's dried. Make sure to keep pets out of the area as well.

Popular Types of Mops & Uses

Dust

Dust mops are for cleaning the floors, walls, ceilings, and light fixtures. These mops either have longer handles or extendable ones. One of the most common is the Swiffer. These allow you to reach cobwebs at the corners of your rooms as well as dusty fans.

Flat

Flat mops are the most popular and most common type of mop. It is used for everyday mopping and usually has a reusable pad attached to it. They are also budget-friendly and easy to store and set up.

String

String mops are popular for their absorbent nature and scrubbing power. They're very affordable. The downside is they're difficult to wash and wring. Maintenance is a bit of a hassle, and they fall apart a lot. Many commercial places like restaurants use these.

Sponge

Has a spongy head and has its own wringer attached to the mop itself. The heads are removable and allow easy rinsing and replacement. These are best for smooth floors like tiles. It can also clean uneven surfaces.

It dries faster than the other types of mops. The downside is you need to take care of them because they tend to become prone to bacteria. You don't want to risk breeding and spreading bacteria all over the house.

Replace the mop head when it's discolored and begins to smell bad.

Strip

These are synthetic stripped-head wet mops. It has a built-in wringer for ease of use. These are easy to use and wring, are as absorbent as cotton, easy to care for, and dry fast. The material used doesn't hold odor as much as a Sponge mop would.

Steam

Steam mops are more advanced and considered an electric appliance. It has a tank that you need to fill up with water and a cleaning solution. The water inside is released as a stream that sprays on the floor. This is the most ideal mop to clean and disinfect.

The downside is it's more expensive than the other mops and is not applicable for all types of floors.

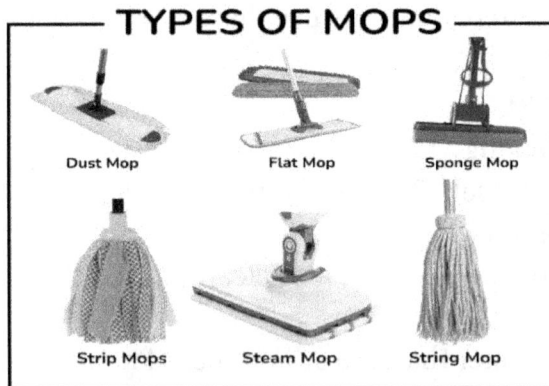

TYPES OF MOPS

Dust Mop   Flat Mop   Sponge Mop

Strip Mops   Steam Mop   String Mop

Cleaning hacks for people with disability, injuries, or mobility restrictions

SAFETY PRECAUTION NEEDED!

SAFETY FIRST

- Always practice safety precautions.
- Do not proceed if you might hurt yourself.
- Request supervision & help if needed.
- Check or test for allergic reactions prior to using any chemicals or ingesting food items.
- If you are injured, too young for the task, or if you have disabilities, you may experience some difficulties doing some specific tasks. Please ask for assistance and guidance when doing the tasks to ensure your overall safety.

Vacuuming

Some vacuum cleaners are quite heavy, making moving them around your home exhausting. A light-weight vacuum is simple to use and transport around the house, making one of the most labor-intensive chores much more manageable. To avoid moving a vacuum up and down stairs, if it's possible, keep a vacuum on each floor of your home.

Dusting

Investing in a duster with a retractable handle will reduce the need to stretch far above furniture, a task that can be exhausting at times.

Take advantage of the dishwasher

A dishwasher not only saves time when it comes to cleaning the dishes, but most of them can also clean plastic items. I regularly will run my small bathroom plastic trashcans, larger trash can lids, and other items that need a deep cleaning, through the dishwasher. It's not just for cereal bowls!

Soak the dishes in hot water

Not everyone has a dishwasher or may prefer to hand wash some or all dishes as a matter of choice. It's a good idea to always rinse off food residue from dishes while the food is still soft and not dried on or set to the dishes.

Another useful household cleaning hack is to soak dishes in hot water for 15 minutes before cleaning them. This will reduce the need to scrub your dishes after cooking. Allow all your kitchen utensils to soak while you eat once you've finished cooking. When you're ready to clean up after your meal, start with the pots, pans, and kitchen utensils, then the rest of your dishes that were just used can be easily washed.

Steam clean the microwave

Heat water in a bowl inside the microwave for three to four minutes. Let the steam produced by the boiling water fill the microwave for a few minutes.

Spray some bleach or anti-bacterial kitchen disinfectant inside the microwave, and then soak it in hot water. Use a clean cloth to remove the dirt after the grime has already been released. With this easy cleaning tip, you may avoid overworking yourself while scrubbing, which frequently happens with those difficult stains.

Let the products do their thing

A quick cleaning tip is to let cleaners sit a few minutes to sink into any dirt after application. This way, the dirt will start to come off the surface without the need for physical scrubbing. This will lessen the power and time required to remove any mold or lime scale by hand. Repeat the procedure and keep the goods on for a longer amount of time if it doesn't work the first time.

Get creative with dryer sheets

The benefits of dryer sheets go well beyond just softening your laundry. Have your pots and pans picked up any stubborn dirt? To help soften the leftover food, soak a non-woven polyester dryer sheet overnight in a pan of hot water. Use a dryer sheet to remove the loosened dirt in the morning. Another tip for keeping your house clean is to use dryer sheets instead of dusting rags to wipe your computer and television displays. Your displays will be clear of dust and fingerprints because of the silicon layer on the dryer sheets, which also reduces static.

You don't have to do all the tasks in one day

While some people prefer to have a cleaning or chores day, others prefer to spread the workload to multiple days to lessen the amount of time needed for housework.

It might be helpful to explain to other family members that by splitting up the responsibilities, you could have more time and energy to spend with them.

Use cleaning tools to make cleanups easier

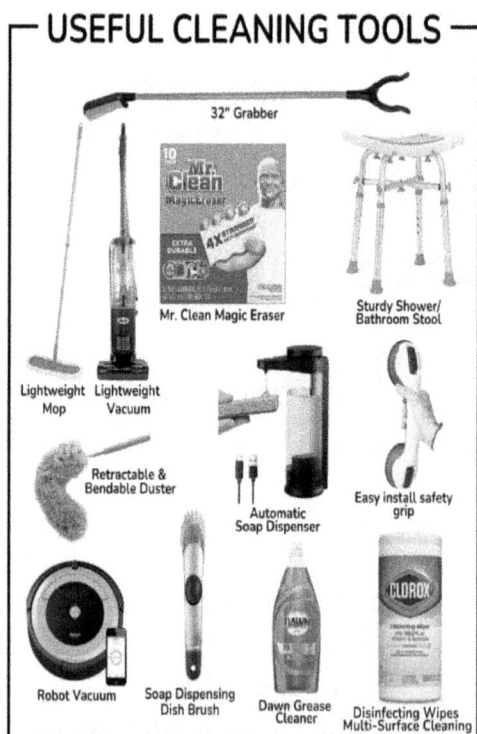

USEFUL CLEANING TOOLS

32" Grabber

Mr. Clean Magic Eraser

Sturdy Shower/Bathroom Stool

Lightweight Mop

Lightweight Vacuum

Retractable & Bendable Duster

Automatic Soap Dispenser

Easy install safety grip

Robot Vacuum

Soap Dispensing Dish Brush

Dawn Grease Cleaner

Disinfecting Wipes Multi-Surface Cleaning

Useful Cleaning Tools

These tools help those with disability or injury to perform cleaning tasks easily and efficiently. Even those without disability can use these tools to hasten cleanup duties.

Grabber - This is an extendable tool that you can use to reach things easily. Buy one that's made for heavy use and can handle heavier weights.

Lightweight Mop - This makes cleanup easier without added stress on your arms and can be carried and used with one hand.

Lightweight Vacuum - This vacuum is more portable and can be lifted and operated using one hand only. It should be light enough to ensure that you won't struggle too much, even when handling it while sitting in a wheelchair.

Mr. Clean Magic Eraser - You may use any generic Magic erasers, but this brand is reportedly most efficient.

Sturdy Shower Stool - Cleanups are hard especially if you must scrub the bathtub, shower area and the floor. These tasks become easier if you use a sturdy shower stool. It's waterproof and anti-slip, so you're sure you won't get into any accidents during your bathroom cleanups.

Easy install safety grip - To avoid slipping and falling down, it's easier if you can hold on to the walls firmly. Unfortunately, walls tend to become slippery if your hands are wet so it's very useful to use a safety grip to help you move around a slippery area.

Automatic Soap Dispenser - This is very convenient because you don't have to carry and pour heavy dishwashing bottles. You can also use this for cleaning solutions, not just for soap.

Retractable, Bendable Duster - You can bend and extend this to reach nooks and crannies and other hard-to-reach areas.

Robot Vacuum - The robot vacuum is programmed to clean the floor and navigate its way around automatically. This is helpful to catch dust and fur while you're doing something else.

Soap Dispensing Dish Brush - This brush is easy to use and will help you clean the dishes without having to pump dish soap every time.

Dawn Grease Cleaner - You can use any cleaner that targets dirt and specifically, grease. This cleaner can be used for other areas around the house to remove mildew, mold, soap stains, etc.

Clorox Disinfecting Wipes (Multi-surface cleaning) - To avoid soap stains, and other dirt and stains, you can use these wipes to immediately clean anything.

Dishwashing

Tools:
Dish Soap - any will do.

Drain rack - These are available in hardware and big box stores.

Plastic net puff scrubber - These work reasonably well and dry quickly, but gunk, particularly cooked egg, has a tendency to get stuck in them.

Dish Brush - They are great for pre-washing the dishwasher or dumping things into the garbage disposal. Find one with a straight edge you can use to scrape if you want one.

Dishcloth - They work well for cleaning counters, and you can wash dishes with them. They are restricted in some ways. If you're not careful, germs can grow on them because they are absorbent. After each use, you must wash them with soap, boil them, or throw them in the microwave to kill any germs.

A dry dish towel or sponge should not be microwaved. You'll ignite a fire. In between uses, you should hang them to dry.

Sponge - In terms of maintenance and use, these are very similar to dishcloths, but they don't dry as quickly, and most sponges will carry bacteria in them. I suggest using it as a one-time project and then disposing of rather than reusing it.

Green scrubber pad - They don't get too much food stuck in them, dry quickly, and scrub well.

Dishwashing Instructions:

Prepare Dishes for Washing

Use a rubber spatula or paper towel to scrape food residue off dishes. Before washing dishes or cookware with food that has stuck to it, soak it in hot water with detergent or baking soda for 15 to 30 minutes. Drain, then move on to Step 2 of the cleaning procedure.

TIP: Avoid pouring grease down the drain because it can clog it. If you forget and pour it down, immediately run hot water through the sink pipes for several minutes to make sure it stays in liquid form as it passes your plumbing system.

Fill

Put hot, clean water and a small amount of soap in the sink or dishpan. You can set some dishes in the water to begin loosening debris.

TIP: If the water gets greasy, too cool, or the suds vanish during the process, drain it and start over.

Wash

Start with the lightly soiled items and wash "in order." Glasses, cups, and flatware are typically included in this.

Plates, bowls, and serving dishes should be washed after these.

Dishes are generally easier if you scrub them while keeping them submerged in water; as you work, pull each dish out from the water to look for missed spots. Save the pots and pans for last. It gives the debris time to loosen more since it may be baked or cooked onto the surface.

You wash in order because you want to use the cleanest water for the items that will sparkle and shine more, like glassware and silverware, leaving pots and pans for the rest of the mostly clean water.

TIP: Knives should never be put into dishwater in advance. Always leave those out, and wash them one at a time, to avoid accidental cutting. To dry, place them, handle side up into a drying rack or flat on a drying towel.

Rinse
Rinse suds with fresh, hot water. Rinse either by placing them in a drying rack and pouring or spraying water over them or by submerging the dishes in a clean sink of water. Remember to rinse the interior of cups, bowls, and glassware.

Dry
It is simpler and more sanitary to air dry than to towel dry. When flatware of glassware is spotted or filmed, however, wiping with a clean towel is beneficial. Make sure the towel is spotless and replace it when it starts to

get damp. Pots and pans can be dried with paper towels, particularly if they have grease residue.

TIP: Remember to tidy up after yourself. It will simplify the task for tomorrow! Wash and dry the dishpan, dish drainer, and sink. Rags, dish towels, and sponges should be washed in the washing machine or left out to dry naturally. Do not forget to frequently replace rags and sponges.

Maintenance

Repair and Maintenance of Lights

This section of the book will assist you in distinguishing between the various types of light bulbs and bases. You'll be able to figure out what kind of bulbs you'll need, what wattages are best, and how to dispose of light bulbs that have broken.

The information here can be used to determine what type of light you need and what your options are. If you were replacing more than a desk lamp, it would be a good idea to request assistance with replacing lights.

How to Replace Lights

Make sure to switch off the power.
One thing that's often overlooked is changing the lights when the power is still on. This is unsafe and could lead to possible shock. Make sure that the light switch is turned to off.

Take safety measures.

One other thing that you should consider is the height of the ceiling of the bulb that needs replacing. You might need a sturdy three or 5-step ladder. Make sure that you will be able to reach the light bulb without endangering yourself. Don't try to balance yourself on a chair that's not steady. You might slip while you're doing the bulb replacement and hurt yourself.

Let the bulb cool off.
Always let the bulb cool off before removing or replacing it. This is because the bulb can become very hot for you to handle. Unless you have thick work gloves that you can use to handle a hot light bulb, do ensure to let it cool off.

Take the bulb out of the socket and replace it with a new one.
Light bulbs are usually released counterclockwise and tightened using a clockwise direction. Try to assess which one of these is true and take note of it. The type of sockets for lighting differs a lot. You must know the type of bulb you need. The next section will discuss the types of bulbs and other considerations needed in selecting a light bulb.

TIP: "Righty tighty, Lefty loosey."

How To Find the Right Light Bulb

You may bring the old light bulb to buy a new one exactly like it. Some incidences require you to change the type of light bulb you need. For example, you want to brighten up your room further. Do you want to lessen the brightness of your desk lamp? Did the old light bulb shatter when you dropped it while attempting to retrieve it?

Most of the time, people throw out old light bulbs and then regret doing so afterward. These are cases where you need to know what type of light bulb you need.

So, how do you find the right light bulb?

1. Determine what fitting or cap type you need

This is the most important information you need to have the correct light bulb that would fit the cap.

Caps and bases of light fixtures have labels on them that use both letters and numbers. The letter indicates what type of base you need.

The number indicates the diameter of the base, which is in millimeters (mm). There may or may not be a third letter that indicates how many pins the bulb should have.

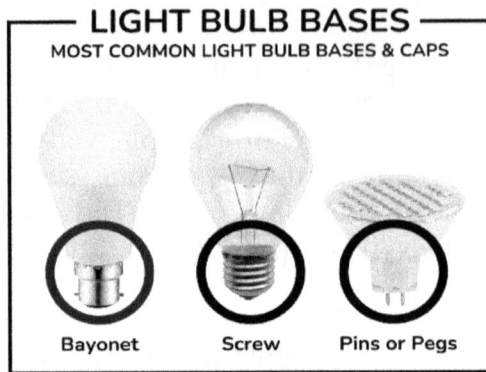

LIGHT BULB BASES
MOST COMMON LIGHT BULB BASES & CAPS

Bayonet   Screw   Pins or Pegs

Here are the most common cap and base types:

a. Bayonet
This is the most common base type in the US & UK. Bulbs are placed into this socket using push and twist action. The most common types of bulbs that use Bayonet bases are CFL bulbs and incandescent bulbs.

b. Screw
Screw bases are also referred to as "Edison" bases. Two wires connect the filament to the base. The base is where electrical voltage connects with and powers the bulb.

c. Pins or Pegs
Pins or Pegs are identifiable by the two narrow pins sticking out of them. The base type code also shows the distance between the pegs or pins in millimeters.

Do you want CFL, Halogen, or LED

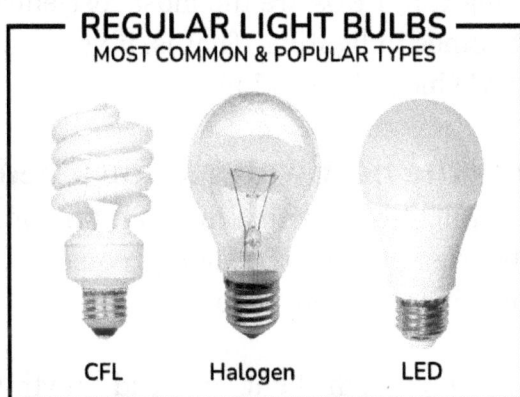

REGULAR LIGHT BULBS
MOST COMMON & POPULAR TYPES

CFL   Halogen   LED

CFL (Compact Fluorescent Lamp)

CFLs are cheaper and have a wide range of sizes and outputs. An advantage is that they are at least four times more efficient than incandescent bulbs. The downside is they are slower to brighten than other types. Also, the light they emit isn't favored by most people.

HALOGEN

Halogen and Incandescent bulbs both use tungsten filament. This makes the color of light they emit very similar. Halogens are more expensive than other similar energy saver light bulbs. The upside is that the life span of halogens is around two years. They also emit a lot of heat.

LEDs (Light Emitting Diodes)

LEDs use 90% less energy than traditional incandescent bulbs. This makes them the most energy-efficient lighting option available. LEDs are more expensive to buy at first, but they can last up to 25 years.

In the long run, LEDs are the most cost-effective option when it comes to lighting. That is, if you compared it to an old-style incandescent bulb.

What is the best wattage for a bedroom?

Look for a light bulb with a lumen rating of 800 or less for a bedroom. This is roughly equal to a 60-watt traditional incandescent bulb.

You'll have enough light to read anything at this brightness level. It will help you feel relaxed when it's time to go to bed. As a rough guide, a bed-sized table lamp should have around 400 lumens. A good-sized living room should have between 1,500 and 3,000 lumens total (from all the bulbs in the room combined).

What Does a Standard Light Bulb Look Like?

In the US, the E26 light bulb is the recommended size. The MES (Medium or Standard) base is used with E26 bulbs.

A base for light bulbs that can be screwed into a light fixture is called an Edison Screw. It bears Thomas Edison's name, who was an inventor. Additionally, there are smaller bulbs like the E12 and E17 as well as bigger bulbs like the E39.

Is the E26 Bulb a Common Bulb?

E26 bulbs are the most common and are considered the STANDARD light bulb. An upside-down pear is a common comparison for the standard "A" bulb form. The two numbers following the letter denote the diameter of the bulb at its widest point.

An A19 bulb has a radius of approximately 1.2 inches, or a diameter of 19 divided by 8 inches. These are for table lamps, floor lamps, ceiling fans, etc. Shapes that use E26 include standard incandescent bulbs, vintage, globe, tubular, and smart bulbs.

What is the difference between an A19 and an E26 light bulb?

They're the same thing. Each number designates a

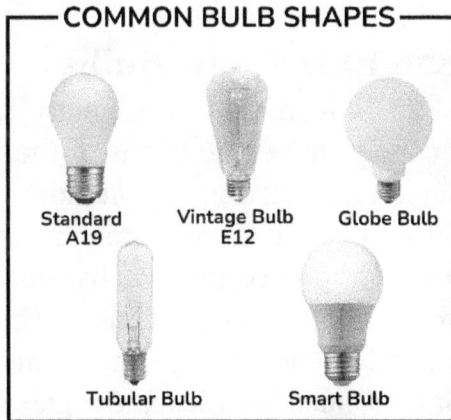

COMMON BULB SHAPES

Standard A19

Vintage Bulb E12

Globe Bulb

Tubular Bulb

Smart Bulb

different area of the bulb. The "A19" refers to the bulb's shape. The "E26" stands for the diameter of the bulb's base.

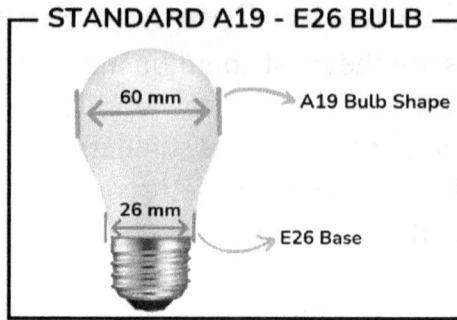

STANDARD A19 - E26 BULB

60 mm — A19 Bulb Shape

26 mm — E26 Base

E26 vs. E27 Bulbs

The main distinction is the thread diameter at the base. The E27 bulb has a diameter of 27 millimeters, while the E26 bulb has a diameter of 26 millimeters. In the United States, E26 bulbs are the standard, whereas E27 bulbs are most common in Europe.

Using E26 LED Smart Bulbs

With an E26 base thread size, smart LED bulbs are simple to use. Because E26 is one of the most common thread diameters, there are a plethora of smart bulb options. Smart LED bulbs are a trend these days because you can use an app to control the lighting. Turn it on or off, use different colors, dim it, use a timer to open or close it, control the light temperature, etc. You must use an app though such as Alexa, Google Assistant, or a specific phone app for the smart bulb.

Brightness

When everyone had incandescent bulbs in their homes, brightness was measured in watts. Watts is a measure of power. It has become less useful as a measure of brightness. This is because of the introduction of energy-saving bulbs like LEDs.

The new bulbs generate the same amount of light with less electricity. Lumens are now used to measure light output. The brighter the light, the higher the lumens.

Wattage and lumen output of the different types of energy-saving bulbs:

WATTS NEEDED TO
GENERATE LUMENS/BRIGHTNESS

BRIGHTNESS	220+	400+	700+	900+	1300+
Incandescent	25W	40W	60W	75W	100W
Halogen	18W	28W	42W	53W	70W
CFL	6W	9W	12W	15W	20W
LED	4W	6W	10W	13W	18W

Get Rid of an Old Light Bulb

Remove the bulb in a safe manner. Keep in mind that light bulbs are vulnerable and fragile. As a result, you don't want to toss them into your garbage can at random. The shards of the bulb can cut and injure someone if it breaks.

Before discarding the old bulb, wrap it in the package of the new bulb. You could also use an old newspaper or magazine to wrap the old bulb. Place the bulb somewhere out of reach of children. If recycling is possible or required in your area, make sure to do so.

SAFETY PRECAUTION NEEDED!

SAFETY FIRST

- Always practice safety precautions.
- Do not proceed if you might hurt yourself.
- Request supervision & help if needed.
- Check or test for allergic reactions prior to using any chemicals or ingesting food items.
- If you are injured, too young for the task, or if you have disabilities, you may experience some difficulties doing some specific tasks. Please ask for assistance and guidance when doing the tasks to ensure your overall safety.

Cooking & Nutrition

Basic Skills & Info That You Should Learn

Cooking involves a lot of skills; it isn't just putting everything in a pot or pan. Cooking also includes knowing the information about the food you'll be using. It includes cleaning, peeling, and cutting to prepare the ingredients you need to cook.

This section will cover the basic information you need to ensure that your cooking skills are useful not just to you but to your parents and siblings.

If you already know how to cook, some information may look too basic, but please understand that not everyone knows all the information needed to be able to cook and prepare ingredients properly. You may even find some useful tips that you can try next time you cook.

The information and instructions found in this chapter are meant for everyone. Some people who have difficulties handling dangerous items such as knives and boiling water should request assistance to avoid getting hurt.

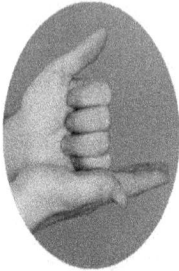

REMINDERS FOR PEOPLE WITH INJURY OR DISABILITY

How to Boil an Egg

Make sure your eggs aren't too cold from the fridge. It will be less of a shock for the egg to reach the hot water if it is at room temperature, and thus less likely to crack.

Place eggs gently on the bottom of a large pot with water covering the top of the eggs. Raise to high heat and let eggs sit in boiling water the proper number of minutes to reach the desired stage boiled egg.

If you're not going to eat the eggs right away, scoop them out of the pan and place them in a bowl containing cold water to stop them from cooking any further.

How long does it take to boil an egg?

EGG YOLK QUALITY

3 minutes
Soft-boiled

5 minutes
For dipping

6 minutes
Medium-boiled

8 minutes
For Scotch egg

10 minutes
Mashable egg

12 minutes
Hard-boiled

Time needed to achieve your desired yolk quality:

- 3 minutes: SOFT-BOILED.
- 5 minutes: set white and runny yolk – perfect for dipping into
- 6 minutes: MEDIUM BOILED.
- 8 minutes: softly set – for Scotch eggs, this is what you want.
- 10 minutes: Mashable hard-boiled egg that isn't dry or chalky.
- 12 minutes: HARD BOILED.

Make an ice bath in a bowl. Remove the cooked eggs from the heat and place them in ice water to cool completely before peeling.

TIPS:

- Use the eggs that have been in the refrigerator the longest for the easiest peeling. The easier it is to peel an egg, the less fresh it is.

- A hard-boiled eggs shell may be peeled by first cracking it all over with a hard surface and then rolling it between your palms to loosen it.

- Peeling should begin at the large end. To help remove the shell, hold the egg under cold running water. You can also place it in a bowl of water.

- In the fridge, hard boiled eggs with the shell on will last for one week if kept in a sealed container.

- Spin an egg to see whether it's hard boiled or raw. It is hard boiled if it spins around evenly. It's a raw egg if it wobbles while spinning.

How To Cook Pasta

1. Use a large pot for cooking the pasta.

Choose a large pot with plenty of room for the pasta to move around in. Break out the eight or twelve quart stockpot.

2. Fill the pot halfway with water.

For a standard 16 oz. package of pasta, you'll need five or six quarts of water. Just as pasta requires a large pot, it also needs a large amount of water to completely submerge each strand.

3. Season the water with salt.

Make it salty! Don't shake the shaker only once; you'll need at least a tablespoon for 6 quarts of water. The salty water enhances the flavor of the pasta.

4. Bring the water to a boil over high heat.

Again, don't let a case of hunger convince you to throw in the pasta when the water is almost simmering.

A vigorous boil is desired. Remember that once you drop the pasta in, the temperature of the water will drop. Replace the lid to speed up the process of bringing the water back to a boil. As soon as you hear the water boiling again, remove the lid. Keep stirring to avoid the pasta from clumping together.

5. To keep the pasta from sticking, stir constantly.

Don't look away and be distracted by the TV or social media. Keep an eye on the pot and stir it at least twice or three times while it's cooking.

Do not allow the strands to clump together.

6. Two minutes before it's "ready," test the pasta.

Check the cook times on the pasta package. Beginning in the earlier range of the time frame, check the pasta for doneness. Using a pasta fork, fish out a single strand of pasta. Allow it to cool before biting into it.

7. Set aside a tablespoon of pasta water.

Scoop out a cup or two in a Pyrex measuring cup or anything that won't crack before draining the water.

This starchy water can be used in sauces to either bind the sauce to the pasta or thin out thick sauces, so they coat the noodles.

8. Drain and toss with pasta sauce before serving.

Drain your pasta in a colander in the kitchen sink. Return the drained pasta to the sauce pot, add the pasta water, and toss to coat evenly. Serve immediately.

SPAGHETTI NOODLES

COOKING TIME TO GET THE RIGHT TEXTURE

al dente **6-7 mins**

chewy **8-10 mins**

soft & chewy **10-12 mins**

mushy **more than 12 mins**

Spaghetti Cooking Time Guide:

6-7 minutes after boiling - Al Dente

8-10 minutes - Chewy and cooked through

10-12 minutes - Chewy but softer

More than 12 minutes - Mushy

TIPS:

- In contrast to dried pasta, fresh pasta cooks quickly, in only two to three minutes. Save it until it is entirely dry since it is more difficult to prepare than dried.
- Pasta that has been filled, like ravioli, will float to the top after it is ready.
- Oil should not be added to the pasta water. Some cooks believe that a squirt of olive oil will keep the strands from clumping together. But that's nothing a good stir can't fix, and the oil may make

your pasta too slick for the sauce to stick to.

- When your pasta is done cooking, don't rinse it. All the starches that bind it to the sauce might get washed away.
- Here's how to get the water to boil faster. Cover the pot with a lid but leave a portion of it uncovered so you can hear when the water begins to boil. Leaving a gap will also help prevent the water from boiling over as you lower the temperature.
- Most dried pasta ribbons, such as spaghetti, linguine, and tagliatelle, take 8-10 minutes to cook.
- Shorter, thicker pasta shapes like penne or bows take 10-12 minutes to cook, whereas tortellini and other fresh pasta take three to five minutes.
- Before mixing the pasta with any sauce or dressing, drain the pasta once it has done cooking and let it steam dry for a few seconds.
- If the sauce you want to use is too thick, keep a little pasta water aside to thin it out.
- Given the fact that cannelloni tubes and lasagna sheets are baked rather than boiled, make sure the sauce you layer or stuff them with isn't too dry, as they will absorb some liquid while baking.
- Separately heat your sauce and then add the cooked pasta to it.

How to Make a Perfect Grilled Cheese Sandwich

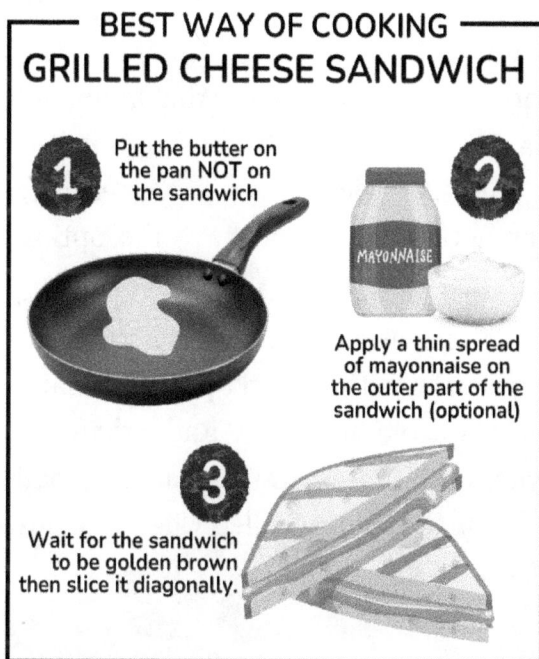

BEST WAY OF COOKING
GRILLED CHEESE SANDWICH

1. Put the butter on the pan NOT on the sandwich

2. Apply a thin spread of mayonnaise on the outer part of the sandwich (optional)

3. Wait for the sandwich to be golden brown then slice it diagonally.

The epitome of craving-worthy food is a grilled cheese sandwich. It is easy and fast to do and it's so yummy. It's easy to do but there are some tips you should know to make the best-grilled cheese sandwich.

The first thing to do is to place the butter on the pan rather than directly on the bread. Instead of butter, spread mayo on the exterior part of the sandwich. Mayo has a higher smoke point compared to butter, which ensures that the sandwich is golden and not burned.

The taste of the mayo will not be apparent because once you cook the bread on the butter placed in the pan, the butter's flavor will dictate the outer flavor of the bread. The spreading of the mayo is optional. If you're not keen on the mayo, you can skip it.

It is critical to choose a cheese that melts well. A piece of young cheddar cheese would be the best option because it has a richer flavor than American Cheese. American cheese is a very popular option but if you have the option to choose young cheddar, go for it.

You'd need a spatula to press down the pan. This helps achieve even levels of toasting. Don't press too hard though. Once you achieve the golden brown and crispy texture, place your sandwich on a plate. Now, cut it diagonally. This cut of the sandwich makes your Grilled Cheese Sandwich taste a whole lot better.

BEST CHEESE TO USE
for GRILLED CHEESE SANDWICHES

American cheese Young Fontina cheese Havarti cheese

Gouda cheese Cheddar cheese

Types of Cheese to be used

1. American cheese

American not only gives you a sandwich with that distinctive orange stripe of melted goo, but it also has a deliciously nostalgic flavor.

2. Young Fontina cheese

Young fontina is better for grilled cheese because it has a softer, smoother texture that melts sweet and creamy.

3. Havarti cheese

Havarti is the result of a cheesemaker's quest for an ultra-creamy cheese in the mid-1800s. It melts smoothly in a grilled cheese sandwich, without the oily separation that other cheeses can cause.

4. Gouda cheese

Choose a gouda that is young to medium-aged, so it is soft and springy (aged goudas tend to be firm). Young gouda has a great nutty, caramel-like flavor and melts beautifully. Stay away from smoked gouda—smoking changes the consistency of the cheese, and it won't melt as well.

5. Cheddar cheese

Young mild cheddars melt faster, but aged sharp cheddars have a stronger flavor. What is the solution? To combine the best of both worlds, use a blend of young and aged cheddar.

How to Make Smoothies

You can make any smoothie using both fresh and frozen ingredients, including any tasty fruits and vegetables.

Ingredients for a 16-ounce smoothie are listed below:
2 cups frozen fruit
1 cup fresh fruit
½ cup liquid
¼ cup yogurt
1-2 Tbsp. sweetener
Add-ins, optional

STEPS:
1. Always start with the liquid. The fact that it will inevitably sink toward the blade doesn't really matter when you add this in. For a creamy smoothie, choose coconut water, filtered water, or any dairy-free milk. Fruit juices should generally be avoided because they contain extra sugar.

2. Add yogurt. Placing this liquid ingredient closest to the blade will help it combine with the other ingredients to its best ability.

3. Add fresh fruit. Fresh bananas, berries, or even an avocado are added at this point.

4. Toss in leafy greens. You should put them nearer the blade because they blend more easily than frozen fruit does.

5. Add frozen fruit. To avoid the blender getting stuck, wait 5–10 minutes after defrosting it before adding it.

6. Toss in add-ins. If you want to add anything extra to your smoothie to boost its nutritional value, do so now.

7. Mix it up! Start the blender on low so that the ingredients will blend gradually. Increase the speed to medium once it starts churning, then blend until the mixture appears smooth and creamy.

Best Blenders for Smoothies

NutriBullet – An excellent personal blender choice. To fit all of the ingredients without exceeding the maximum fill line, use the larger cup.

Vitamix – The most potent of the conventional blenders, the Vitamix will always produce a silky-smooth smoothie. Only invest in this if you frequently make smoothies, soups, or sauces because it is more of a luxury.

Food Processor – If you don't have access to another blender, you could try using a food processor as a sort of last resort.

Ingredients You Need for Basic Smoothies

Strawberry Banana
- 1 cup strawberries (fresh or frozen)

1 frozen banana
- ½ cup unsweetened Greek yogurt
- 1 cup unsweetened milk (nut, animal, soy)

Tropical Smoothie
- ½ cup pineapple (fresh or frozen)

½ frozen banana
- ½ cup mango (fresh or frozen)
- ½
- cup unsweetened Greek yogurt
- ½ an orange, peeled
- ½ cup ice (not necessary if using frozen pineapple and mango)
- 1 cup unsweetened milk (nut, animal, soy)

Very Berry Smoothie
- 1
- cup mixed frozen berries (either fresh or frozen)
- 1 frozen banana
- ½ cup unsweetened Greek yogurt
- 1 cup unsweetened milk (nut, animal, soy)

Peanut Butter Smoothie
- 1 frozen banana
- 1 tablespoon peanut butter
- ½ cup unsweetened Greek yogurt
- 1 cup unsweetened milk (nut, soy, animal)

Chocolate Peanut Butter Smoothie

- 1 frozen banana
- 1 tablespoon peanut butter
- 1 tablespoon cocoa powder
- ½ cup unsweetened Greek yogurt
- 1 cup unsweetened milk (nut, soy, animal)
- Sweetener to taste

Cherry Pomegranate Detox Smoothie

- ½ a frozen banana
- ½ cup sour cherries
- ½ cup pomegranate seeds (arils)
- ½ cup ice
- 1 cup unsweetened milk (nut, soy, animal)

Green Goddess Smoothie

- ½ a frozen banana
- ½ cup green grapes
- 1 kiwi, peeled
- 1 cup baby spinach leaves
- ½ cup ice
- 1 cup unsweetened milk (nut, soy, animal)

Extra Green Smoothie

- ½ a frozen banana
- ½ cup blueberries, fresh or frozen
- ½ an orange, peeled
- 1 to 2 cup baby kale and/or baby Swiss chard
- ½ cup ice
- 1 cup unsweetened milk (nut, soy, animal)

Cut and Peel Garlic

How to easily peel a garlic bulb

Choosing a good, firm garlic bulb is the first step in chopping garlic. Here are some ways to peel a clove of garlic. Choose one that you're most comfortable with and suits your needs.

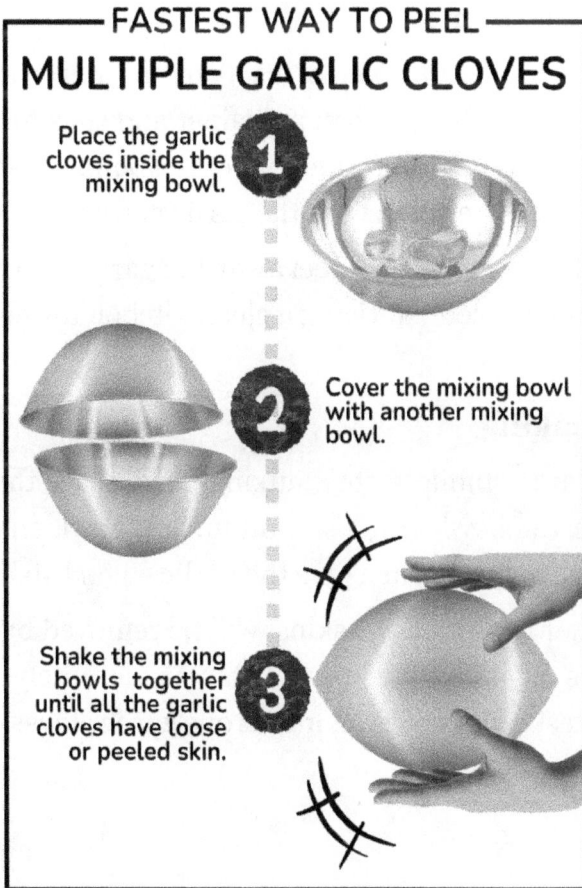

FASTEST WAY TO PEEL
MULTIPLE GARLIC CLOVES

Place the garlic cloves inside the mixing bowl.
1

Cover the mixing bowl with another mixing bowl.
2

Shake the mixing bowls together until all the garlic cloves have loose or peeled skin.
3

1. Crush garlic slightly

The garlic clove should be laid flat on the chopping board. With your palm softly pressed over it, place the flat side of a knife over it. Do this until you feel the squish and hear the slight crushing sound. Remove the knife from the table. The papery skin can be easily peeled off once it has been loosened.

2. Boil water

In a medium saucepan, bring a pot of water to a boil. Place the unpeeled garlic cloves in a strainer and soak for 20 seconds in hot water. Get the strainer out of the boiling water and place it in an ice-water bath with the garlic cloves.

Cut the root ends and peel away the garlic skins as soon as the cloves have cooled. Using a clean kitchen towel, pat dry.

3. Shaking

In a large stainless-steel mixing bowl, place the garlic cloves. Cover the bowl with a second mixing bowl, ensuring that the edges are flush. Then give the garlic a good shake.

Most, if not all, of the skins, will be removed by slamming the cloves against the bowls. This is definitely the best and quickest way of peeling numerous garlic cloves.

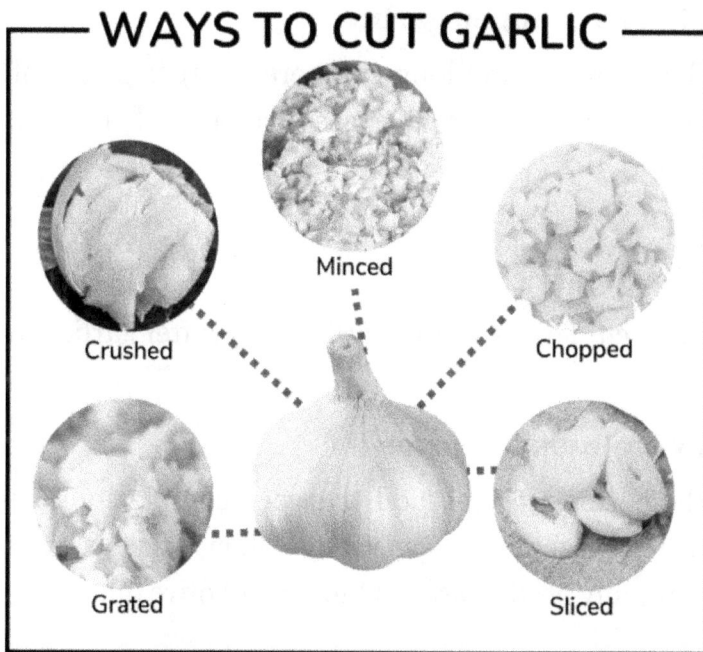

WAYS TO CUT GARLIC

Crushed

Minced

Chopped

Grated

Sliced

How to Cut Garlic & Its Uses

1. Crushed garlic

Using a garlic clove press or mortar and pestle to crush garlic is a great way to make salad dressings or sauces. They are easier to incorporate into the other ingredients and provide the most flavor.

2. Small minced garlic

The finer the mince, the more flavor-packed juices are released, resulting in a stronger garlic flavor. Salads, pesto, and salsas benefit a lot from raw, minced garlic. It gives them a slight kick with regards to the flavor.

3. Large chopped garlic

When sautéed and long-simmered, larger pieces of chopped garlic heat up and evenly season a batch of chili, pasta sauce, or soup.

4. Garlic slices

Thinly cut large slices of garlic add a softer garlic flavor.

5. Whole garlic cloves

Whole garlic cloves add a sweet complexity to purées of roasted vegetables, especially when roasted. They're also commonly used to season butter and olive oil.

6. Grated garlic

You can grate a piece of garlic bulb using a cheese grater. This is one of the best techniques because you can grate a whole lot of garlic all at once! Place all the grated garlic inside a small empty bottle. Place it inside your refrigerator and get only what you need. It makes cooking and preparation faster.

How to cut garlic cloves

Place the peeled garlic clove on its side, flatter side down. Keep one hand on top of the blade as you carefully move the knife over the clove from left to right, slicing to the desired thickness. These thin slices of garlic can be used to add a subtle flavor to cooked dishes or pickle brines.

How do I keep unused garlic safe?

The rest of the bulb should be kept at room temperature in a paper bag because garlic thrives in a dark, ventilated environment. When stored in a dry, ventilated container in a cool, dark location like a pantry shelf, whole bulbs can last for months.

The rest of the bulb, however, is only good for seven to ten days after a clove has been removed. In the fridge, tightly wrapped peeled cloves will last a week, and tightly wrapped cut garlic will last a day or two. But keep in mind that whole garlic bulbs should not be refrigerated.

The humidity in the refrigerator makes the bulbs mushy, which can lead to sprouting.

How To Freeze Garlic

Freezing garlic is very convenient since you won't have to keep on preparing garlic whenever you need it. Each batch is good for 3 months up to 6 months.

It also saves money because it's way cheaper than buying jarred garlic. It tastes better too!

1. Clean and Peel 4-5 cups of garlic. You can either use a blender for 1 minute OR you can use a grater and grate the garlic cloves.

2. Add 1 teaspoon of salt for every 4-5 cups of garlic cloves. If adding oil, add up to ½ cup oil.

3. Blend or mix well until it has a paste consistency.

4. Use Ziplock storage bags for the garlic paste. Flatten and use a ruler or the backside of a knife to push down on the Ziplock bag to divide the contents inside into layers for easier handling.

5. Place the Ziplock bags in the freezer.

6. There is no need to thaw the garlic. Just use it as it is. It's great for recipes where the texture of the garlic isn't as important.

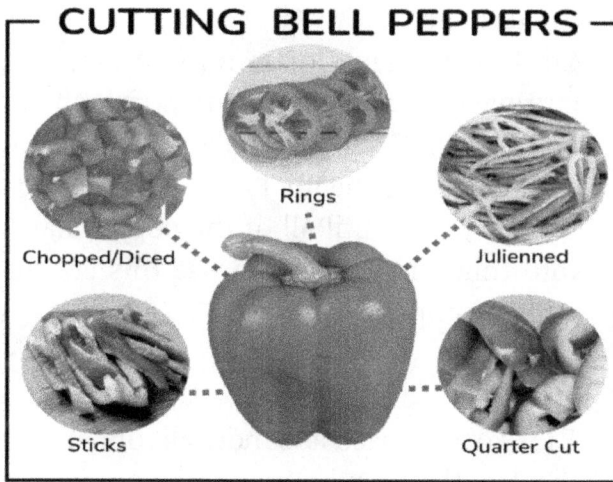

CUTTING BELL PEPPERS

Chopped/Diced

Rings

Julienned

Sticks

Quarter Cut

Cut A Bell Pepper

1. Clean your bell pepper by rinsing it thoroughly under running water and patting it dry with a paper towel.
2. Cut off the top and bottom of the pepper.
3. Put the pepper on the bottom and look for the lines that connect the inner parts to the outer skin of the pepper. The pepper should be cut into four pieces.
4. Remove the stem and seedy core from the trimmed top and throw it away.
5. Proceed to cutting the bell peppers.

- **Sticks**
  To make the sticks, cut each quarter lengthwise into 3-4 sticks.
- **Diced**
  To dice, slice into sticks, then cross-slice the sticks to make dice. They are also components in stews and soups.

- **Julienned**
  Start slicing lengthwise on one piece at a time, cutting each piece into thin strips about half an inch wide. Each piece should be cut with the pepper skin facing up. Repeat with each quartered pepper piece until all of the pepper has been cut into thin strips. You can use this cut for salads, wraps, or appetizers.

- **Rings**
  Rings can be used as sandwich toppers. For a bold display, they can be fried in an air fryer or added to ratatouilles or chilis.

- **Quarter Cut**

Make sure your bell pepper is thoroughly washed with cold water before you begin cutting it. Place the Pepper on a chopping board and, using a sharp knife, slice down each side of the Pepper to quarter it.

Grilled peppers are simple to make. Cut your peppers into quarters. Cover them in olive oil or you're your preferred seasonings and place them skin side down on your grill.

When the peppers are nicely charred and tender, serve them as a flavorful side dish, chopped and added to a salad, or sliced to top a juicy burger.

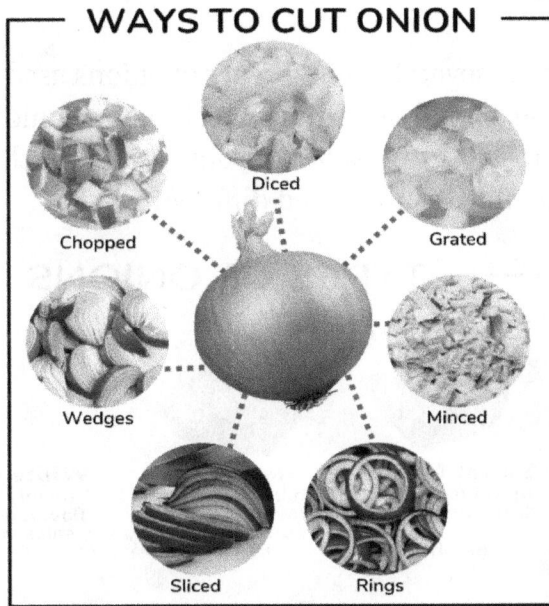

WAYS TO CUT ONION

Diced

Chopped

Grated

Wedges

Minced

Sliced

Rings

Peel & Cut Onion Without Crying

1. Cut the top and Bottom of the onion. Note that when you cut an onion's roots, you will feel teary-eyed. To avoid this, upon cutting the onion's roots, place the onion in a bowl of water while you work on the other onions. The water keeps the chemicals from the onion from making you cry.

2. Cut the onion vertically in half

3. Peel off the first layer of onion skin.

4. Wash the onion and continue cutting as desired.

Types of Onion

There are several popular types of onions used in cooking and you should determine which type of onion to use in order to get the most out of your recipes. Each type has a distinct flavor and is used differently.

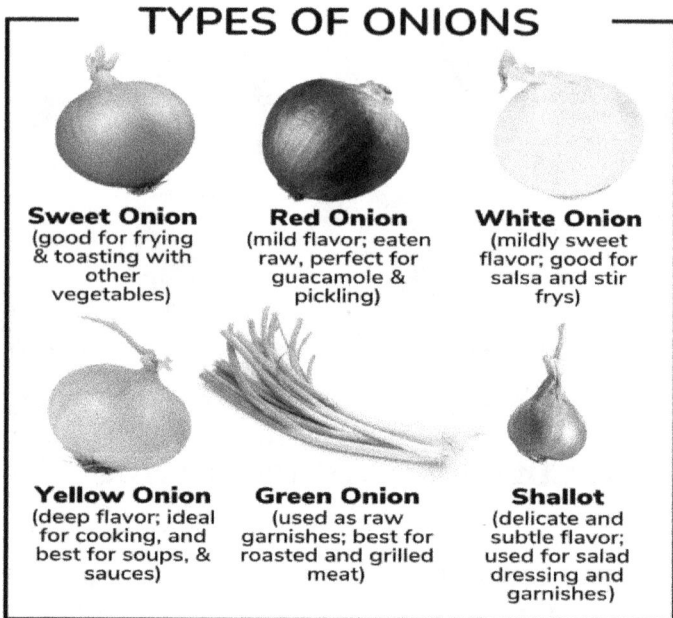

TYPES OF ONIONS

Sweet Onion
(good for frying & toasting with other vegetables)

Red Onion
(mild flavor; eaten raw, perfect for guacamole & pickling)

White Onion
(mildly sweet flavor; good for salsa and stir frys)

Yellow Onion
(deep flavor; ideal for cooking, and best for soups, & sauces)

Green Onion
(used as raw garnishes; best for roasted and grilled meat)

Shallot
(delicate and subtle flavor; used for salad dressing and garnishes)

How to Cut Onion & Its Uses

1. Chopped

Onions should be slightly larger than diced pieces when chopped. It's usually used for soups, salads, and buttered vegetables.

2. Diced

This is the most common cut. Small, uniformly sized cubes of diced onions cook quickly and evenly. Cutting food into cubes of a specific size is referred to as dice. Sauces, toppings, and condiments like tomato relish can all be made with 1/4-inch pieces. In chunky salsas and toppings, 1/2-inch pieces work well. Salads, stews, and soups are commonly made with large 3/4-inch cubes.

3. Grated

Using a regular grater, grate the onion. You can make small onion pieces that caramelize quickly and evenly by grating them. It is suitable for sautéed mixtures.

4. Minced

Minced is the smallest cut for onions. Cut onions into 1/8-inch pieces as finely as possible. This can be used in any recipe that calls for a lot of onion flavor but not the chewy texture of larger pieces.

5. Rings

The best way to make homemade fried onion rings is to cut onions into rings. They're also delicious in roasts or soups.

6. Sliced

Sliced onions can be eaten raw in salads, used to garnish burgers, or may be used to make caramelized onions.

7. Wedges

Cutting an onion into four equal-sized wedges, first vertically and then horizontally, yields onion wedges.

Clean, peel, and cut Ginger
Cleaning

Clean the ginger by soaking it in water and rubbing it thoroughly. Then either pat it dry with a kitchen towel or leave it to dry on the kitchen counter.

Peeling

Peel the skin off with the back of a spoon. If you're having trouble, soak the piece of ginger for a few minutes in warm water to soften the skin. If you need to remove the skin quickly, use the peeler.

Ways to Cut Ginger

1. **Sliced:** Slice the ginger into rounds with a chef's knife and a sharp knife. Ginger should be sliced across the grain of the fibers.

2. **Julienne:** Stack 2-3 of the rounds, then cut to make thin lengthwise sticks.

3. **Chopped:** Arrange the ginger sticks you cut earlier in a straight line and chop them into small pieces.

4. **Minced:** Using a chef's knife, finely chop the ginger pieces. To mince the ginger, move the knife from right to left and vice versa until it becomes much smaller.

5. **Grated:** Hold one end of the ginger and slide it down the grater.

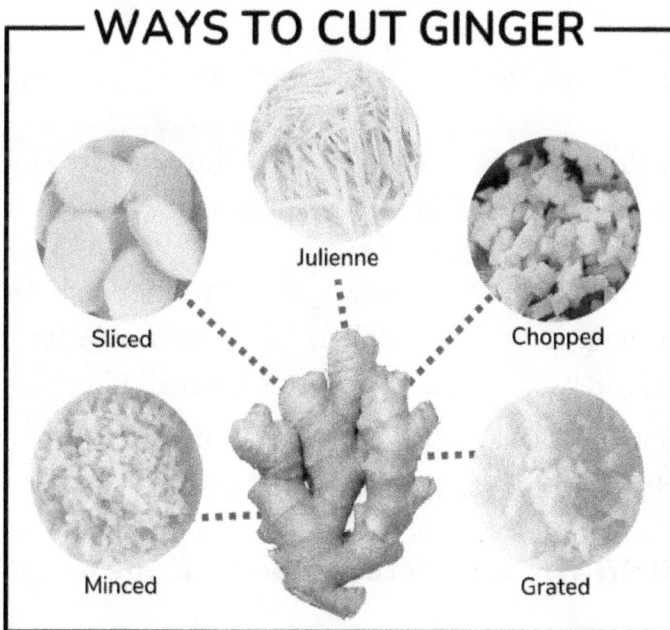

WAYS TO CUT GINGER

Sliced

Julienne

Chopped

Minced

Grated

How to Cook a Steak
Instructions

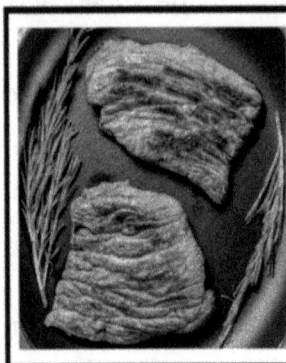

Ingredients:
1 - 2 boneless ribeye or scotch fillet, 2.5 cm thick
1 tbsp vegetable oil
Salt and pepper
5 tbsp unsalted butter cut into 1.25cm
6 sprigs fresh thyme (alternative: 3 sprigs rosemary)
5 garlic cloves, peeled and crushed.

1. Bring to room temperature by removing the steak from the fridge 30 minutes before serving to allow it to be at room temperature.

2. Remove moisture. Use a paper towel, pat the steaks dry.

3. Preheat the skillet. In a heavy-bottomed frypan set over high heat, heat the oil until it is burning hot.

4. Season the steak using salt and pepper on both sides before placing it in a hot skillet. Cook each side for two to three minutes, or until a nice crust is formed. Flip.
Spread Garlic butter on a different pan. After a minute, toss steaks with butter, garlic, and thyme.

WARNING: If there is moisture, the oil will splatter.

5. Baste: As soon as the butter has melted, keep spooning it over the steak until it's cooked to your liking. Total time and

temperature depend on your cooked meat preference.

6. Rest for 5 to 10 minutes after transferring the steak to a plate and covering it loosely with foil. Drizzle butter from the skillet over the steak before serving.

Below is the internal temperature needed to achieve the doneness of steaks.

DONENESS OF STEAK — INTERNAL TEMPERATURE		
Physical Appearance	Doneness	Temperature Range
	Rare	47°C/117°F
	Medium Rare	52°C/126°F
	Medium	57°C/135°F
	Medium Well Done	60°C/140°F
	Well Done	65°C/149°F

How to Cut a Whole Chicken

Below is a representation of where to cut the chicken to yield 8 pieces. This is the most common cut for chicken.

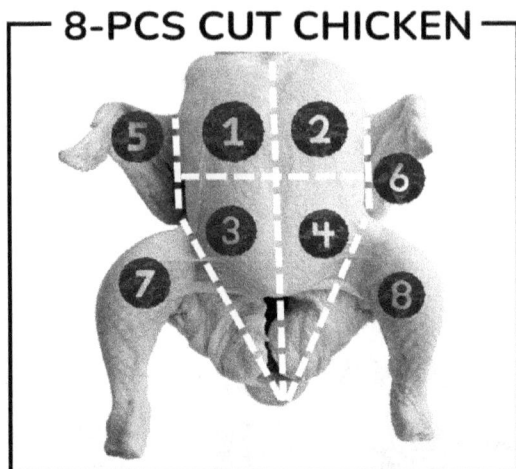

It is very easy to cut chicken. Here's a step-by-step direction on how to cut a whole chicken.

Instructions

1. **Remove the innards and any excess fat from the bird's opening.**

   - Thoroughly rinse the chicken.
   - Drain the chicken on a clean chopping board lined with paper towels.
   - Turn your chicken breasts over to the other side.

HOW TO CUT WHOLE CHICKEN
8-PIECES

Remove the
innards and any
excess fat.

Grasp the thigh-leg
joint and cut
through it.

Cut and take out
the spine.

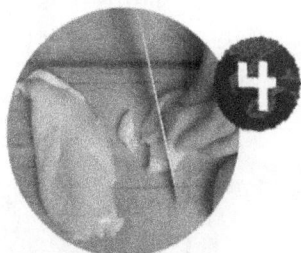

Cut breast part into
4 parts.

Cut the backbone
off and throw it
away.

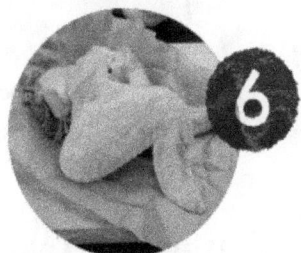

Cut the wings part.

137

2. Cutting the Thigh and Legs.

- At the joint, cut the thighs and legs away.
- Slice the skin between the drumstick & the body using a knife.

- With your hands, locate the joint and pop it out of its socket.
- To remove the leg from the body, finish the cut.
- Grasp the thigh-leg joint and cut through it. You can also pop this joint out of its socket with your hands first.
- Whole chicken legs can be further cut into drumstick & thigh parts. The white line shows where you should cut it.

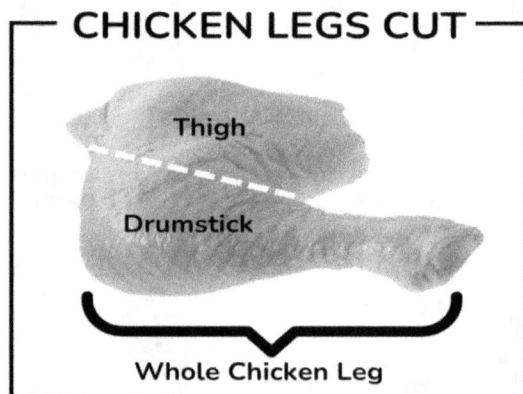

CHICKEN LEGS CUT

Thigh

Drumstick

Whole Chicken Leg

3. Cutting and Taking Out the Spine.

- Take out the spine. Using a sharp knife, cut down each side of the ribs.

- Continue cutting until the spine is completely removed.

TIP: This is a fantastic piece to keep in mind for making chicken stock!

4. Cutting the Breast

- Breasts should be separated. Cut the breast in half by placing the knife on the breastbone and applying pressure. If you have poultry shears or very sharp kitchen scissors, this is a good option.
- Cut the breast in half along the breastbone with poultry shears or sharp kitchen scissors.
- If you're going to use shears, slightly open the chicken and turn it breast-side down. Along one side of the backbone, make a cut.

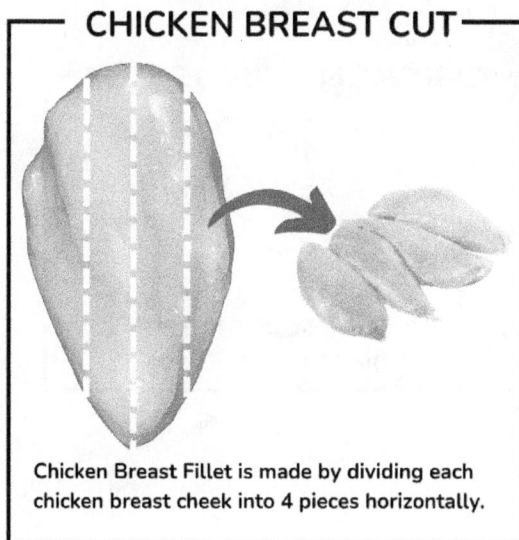

CHICKEN BREAST CUT

Chicken Breast Fillet is made by dividing each chicken breast cheek into 4 pieces horizontally.

- The half of a chicken breast can be referred to as one cheek. One cheek can be divided into four pieces to create a chicken breast filet.

5. **Cut the remaining side of the backbone off and throw it away.**

6. **Cutting the Wings**

   - Using a knife or poultry shears, remove and separate the wings. It's important to remember to cut where the joint is.

   - Once you have the chicken wings, you can further cut each wing into three parts, the drumette, wingette, and tip. Below is a sample of where to cut the wing to produce the three parts.

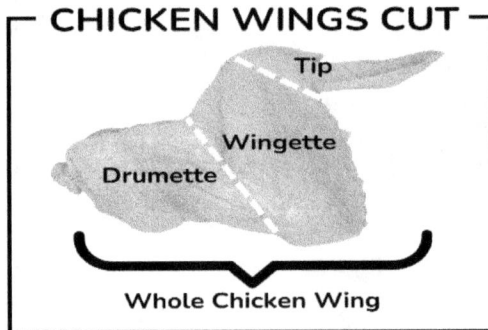

CHICKEN WINGS CUT

Tip

Wingette

Drumette

Whole Chicken Wing

Mashed Potatoes

Ingredients

8 to 10 medium russet potatoes, quartered and peeled (approximately 3 lb.)
1 teaspoon kosher salt
2 tablespoons butter (optional)
a pinch of black pepper
1/4 cup warm milk

In a large saucepan or cooking pot, place the potatoes and enough water to cover them. Toss in 3/4 teaspoon of salt. Bring the water to a boil. Reduce to medium-low heat, cover loosely, and cook for 17 to 20 minutes, or until potatoes can easily break apart when pierced with a fork. Drain thoroughly.

Return potatoes to the saucepan and gently shake for 1 to 2 minutes.

Crush the potatoes with a potato masher until no lumps remain. Continue mashing potatoes with butter, pepper, and the remaining 1/4 teaspoon salt, gradually adding enough milk to make them smooth and creamy.

Tip 1: Use a sturdy potato masher with a flat metal grid-like masher to smash them up quickly and evenly.

Tip 2: Russet potatoes are ideal for mashed potatoes because they're starchy and fall apart easily during cooking, which is ideal for easy mashing.

Tip 3: The easiest way to finish a big bowl of fluffy spuds is with fresh thyme leaves, flaky salt, and lots of freshly ground pepper.

Tip 4: Want an easier version? Whipped potatoes uses a hand mixer or stand mixer to take all the work out of mashing, removes lumps and gives your potatoes a lighter, airy consistency.

Tip 5: Instead of milk, use chicken broth for a great depth of flavor.

Sauté Vegetables

The word "sauté" is derived from the verb "sauter," which means "to jump" in French. When food is cooked in a hot pan with oil, it jumps around a little bit. Sautéing something means quickly cooking it in a shallow pan with a small amount of oil over high heat.

Cooking fats such as avocado oil or vegetable oil are excellent choices. Because butter has a low smoke point, it will burn in the pan before the food has a chance to cook. It's best to save it for a lower-temperature finish.

1. Get the vegetables ready. To ensure that they cook evenly, try to make them the same size. Smaller pieces will cook more quickly.

2.Preheat the frying pan. Pour in enough oil to coat the pan's bottom. Place one piece of vegetable in the oil to test the heat. It's hot enough if it sizzles.

3. Add the vegetables. Arrange the vegetables in one layer in the hot pan. If you overcrowd the pan, the vegetables will steam rather than sauté. Cook until the surface is seared and caramelized.

4. Check the browning on the other side.

5. It's best if the vegetables are still crisp when you serve them. Meat and poultry can be sautéed in the same way.

Air Fryers

PARTS OF AN AIR FRYER

Digital Control

Time Control Knob

Frying Basket

Crumb Basket

Basket Handle

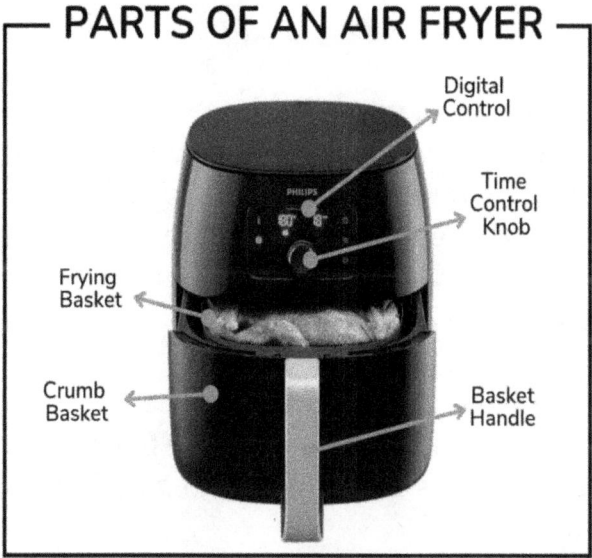

What is an air fryer?

The air fryer is essentially a high-powered countertop convection oven that cooks your food without actually frying it. It mimics the results of deep-frying using only hot air and little or no oil.

What is the process of using an air fryer?

Both a fan and a heating mechanism are housed in the top section of an air fryer. When you turn on the fryer, hot air rushes down and goes around the food in a fryer-style basket.

The food becomes crisp because of the fast circulation, which is the same to deep-frying but without the oil.

An air fryer can be used in the following ways:

1. Fill the basket with your food.
The basket's capacity is anywhere from 2 to 10 quarts, depending on the size of your air fryer. Usually, 1 or 2 teaspoons of oil will be needed to help the food become crispy. In an air fryer, you can use foil to make cleanup a little easier if you're in a hurry.

2. Decide on a time and a temperature.
Depending on the food you're cooking, air fryer cooking times and temperatures range from 5 to 25 minutes at 350° to 400°F.

3. Allow the food to cook.
To help the food crisp up evenly, you may need to flip or turn it halfway through the cooking time. It's critical to clean your air fryer after you've finished cooking.

4. Use heat protection.
Make sure you always have heat protection for your hands and face when you're working with heated goodies!

Make a Vegetable Soup

What Do You Need?

Almost any vegetable can be put into a vegetable soup. Get creative by seeing what you have in your kitchen, or a preferred flavor combination like sweet potato, zucchini, squash, tomato, celery, mushroom, onion, leek, cabbage, kale, chard, potato, rutabaga, cauliflower, broccoli... you get it!

The only thing needed is that you must enjoy the vegetable's flavor. You can mask the bitterness of turnips with cream or yogurt and offset the aroma of cabbage with creamy white beans or tart lemon, but you can't completely mask the taste of a vegetable in soup, so don't add anything you don't like.

Vegetables and stock are required, as well as olive oil or butter and salt and pepper.

147

After that, everything is up to you.

Start with aromatics, such as onion, garlic, or leeks, and some fresh herbs. Smoked salt or spices like cumin or curry powder can be used to season the vegetables.

To make it more interesting, add some diced tomatoes, white beans, chickpeas, or parmesan cheese. Get creative!

Ingredients
Aromatics, such as onion, garlic, or leeks
1 to 2 pounds vegetables
Olive oil or unsalted butter
4 to 6 cups low-sodium stock or broth
Salt and pepper

Needed:
Chopping board
Chef's knife
4-quart (or bigger) pot or Dutch oven, with cover
Wooden spoon

INSTRUCTIONS
1. Prepare 1 to 2 pounds of vegetables. I chose the ones that expected to be consumed as soon as possible: a small head of cauliflower and carrots.

2. Cut the vegetables and aromatics into small pieces. I cut the trimmed cauliflower and unpeeled carrots into chunks that were evenly sized. 1 leek and 2 garlic cloves were also chopped.

3. Warm the olive oil. Heat 1 tablespoon of olive oil over medium heat.

4. Aromatics should be sautéed. Start by cooking the leeks and garlic in the oil until fragrant and soft, about 5 minutes.

5. Cook the vegetables until they are brown. Add the chopped carrot and cauliflower and cook for another few minutes. The vegetables should soften.

6. Season the vegetables using salt and pepper, and add any other seasonings, such as spices or dried herbs, now so they can flavor the soup from the bottom up. Season to taste. You can start with half teaspoon cumin, chili powder, and smoked.

7. Pour in the broth. Bring 4 to 6 cups of broth to a low simmer.

8. Cover and cook on low heat. Minimize the heat to a low setting and cover the pot. Allow for 30 minutes of cooking time before checking the soup. Continue to cook the vegetables until they fall apart if you want them to be very soft for puréeing.

9. Season to taste. Make sure to taste the soup as you work, whether you leave the vegetables whole or purée them.

Choose A Ripe Banana

BANANA RIPENESS

GREENish BANANA
- Starchy
- Greater Satiety
- Source of Prebiotics
- Good for those experiencing Loose Bowel Movement.
- Do not eat when constipated

USED FOR:
Stews
Curries
Casseroles
Deep-fried

YELLOW BANANA
- Sweeter
- Digests Faster
- Source of Antioxidants
- Can be eaten even when constipated

USED FOR:
Fruit salad
Fruit tart toppings
Bread
Rice Pudding

BROWNish BANANA
- Super Sweet
- Greatest Vitamins and Mineral Loss
- Highest Antioxidant Levels

USED FOR:
Ice Cream
Cheesecake
Smoothies
Broiled
Grilled
Pancakes
Waffles

150

Choose an Apple

MOST POPULAR APPLES

Red Delicious
Uses: Eating
Available: Year-round
Taste: Slightly Sweet

Honey Crisp
Uses: Eating, Salad,
Pie, Baking
Available: Sept-Feb
Taste: Sweet & Juicy

Granny Smith
Uses: Eating
, Salad, Baking, Pies,
Sauteing
Available: Year-round
Taste: Sweet & Tart

Gala
Uses: Eating, Apple
Sauce, Pies, Baking,
Saute.
Available: Sept-June
Taste: Very Sweet

McIntosh
Uses: Eating Salad,
Apple Sauce, Apple
Butter
Available: Sept-June
Taste: Sweet, Juicy

Fuji
Uses: Eating, Salad,
Baking, Pies, Apple
Sauce
Available: Year-round
Taste: Very Sweet

Cortland
Uses: Eating, Salad, Apple Sauce,
Apple Butter, Baking, Pies
Available: Sept-April
Taste: Sweet, Slightly Tart, Juicy

How To Identify GMO Food Products

Not many are aware that there are codes to differentiate fruits and vegetables between organic and inorganic or genetically modified.

By reading the label or sticker number on the produce, you can figure out how it was grown. The label or sticker number is called PLU or Price Look Up Code. It helps make inventory control easier and more accurate. It's used for bulk produce such as fruits and vegetables.

- A four-digit number indicates that the food was grown in a conventional manner.
- Produce with a 5-digit number that starts with a 9 is organic.
- A 5-digit number that begins with an 8 indicates that it has been genetically modified.

You can manually check what the PLU Codes really mean by searching for it at https://www.ifpsglobal.com/PLU-Codes.

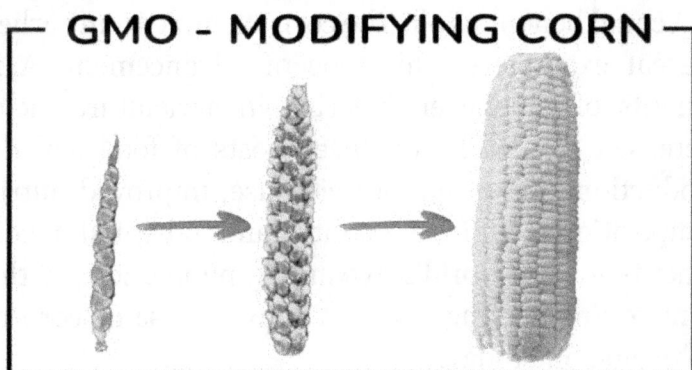

GMO - MODIFYING CORN

Advantages and Disadvantages of GMO

Genetically modified organism (GMO) produce is common and needed because if this isn't done, we won't be able to enjoy certain foods. Corn, for instance, looked like wheat and was so small for it to be eaten. It was then modified; it became larger and is now edible. Thanks to genetic modification.

The potential development of allergens to GM-related crops and toxicity from GM crops are the two most notable Genetically Modified Organism (GMO) risks to humans. GM crops, on the other hand, have been shown in studies to have advantages, such as increased nutritional value in foods. Though the increased nutritional value is lauded, the potential negative consequences are concerning. Toxicity is an example of a negative effect. Possible Allergic Reactions, Antibiotic Resistance, Cancer, and Nutritional Loss are all risks associated with genetically engineered foods.

However, it's worth noting that if we don't support GMOs, we're effectively shutting out potential food items that could benefit us all. The corn example from earlier is a great example of this type of advancement. A few benefits of genetic engineering in agriculture include increased crop yields, reduced costs of food and drug production, decreased pesticide use, improved nutrient composition and food quality, and potential medical benefits for the world's expanding population. Without Genetic Engineering, we won't have the same corn that we're enjoying today.

How to Make a Salad

STEP 1: Combine two or three types of lettuce.

Lettuce is the most important component of a green salad. Lettuce alone is insufficient for a salad. Using only one type of lettuce in a salad can be monotonous. You need to have at least different types and other ingredients to create a good salad.

At the start of a meal, salads are often served, so they should stimulate your appetite while also awakening your taste buds.
 Using different lettuce varieties to highlight contrasting flavors, textures, and colors is one way to accomplish this.

Iceberg, red leaf, green leaf, and romaine lettuce are the most common types of lettuce used in salads. A good salad rule of thumb is to include at least two of these ingredients. Try one that's leafier and one that's a little crunchier.

Because it's leafy on one end and crunchy on the other, Romaine is a particularly versatile vegetable. For second lettuces, bibb, arugula, frisée, and even fresh spinach are excellent choices.

To add contrast, toss in a handful of bagged salad greens. Even though most prepackaged salad greens are already washed, checking for bugs is still a good idea.

STEP 2: Chop the Lettuce into Small Pieces
How to prepare the greens is another aspect of the lettuce equation. Cut your lettuce into small bite-size pieces. There's no reason not to cut the greens with a knife. Just be careful. Handling knives are considered a skill for a reason. Chopped lettuce has nice clean edges, and it's much easier to get uniform-sized pieces with a knife than it is with tearing.

STEP 3: Think About Tomatoes
Take into consideration the time of year and the type of tomato you're using. Classic hothouse tomatoes are a good option, but they're heavy and watery, and they can add a lot of liquid to a salad. Cherry tomatoes are far superior; cut them in half before using them. Trying to eat a whole cherry tomato with a fork is a pain. When it comes to slicing tomatoes, a serrated knife is ideal.

STEP 4: Equalize Your Ingredients

A good salad has the perfect texture, flavor, and color balance. A green salad should include one or two additional vegetables in addition to the lettuce and tomatoes to keep it manageable. Sliced red onion is a good choice because it adds color, crunch, and pungency to the dish. As a backup, try using sliced cucumbers, shredded carrot, shredded cabbage, or sliced bell peppers. Also, aim for a variety of colors, flavors, and textures. Try orange or yellow bell peppers to increase variety.

Finally, rather than chopping your salad vegetables into small pieces, slice or shred them into bite-sized strips. When you toss the salad, diced vegetables tend to sink to the bottom, whereas strips and shreds are more likely to stay distributed throughout.

STEP 5: Maintain a Cool and Crisp Environment
It's critical to have crisp lettuce. Of course, crispness is related to freshness, but how you store your lettuce will determine how long it remains crisp.

Refrigerate it, covered in damp paper towels, in a salad spinner basket or colander. Air circulation is necessary for salad greens. Sealing them in plastic bags will cause them to wilt more quickly.

Another no-no is wet greens. Your salad dressing will simply slide off the leaves and pool at the bottom of the bowl if your lettuce is dripping wet.

A chilled green salad is recommended. Wilted greens are warm greens. And serving your greens on a warm plate is one of the quickest ways to warm them up.

Toss your salad plates in the freezer for a few minutes. It's simple! They will be nice and cool when you're ready to serve if you put them in the fridge for about 30 minutes. Your salad, as well as your guests, will be grateful.

STEP 6: Some Assembly Required

Drizzle the dressing over the salad and put it gently. If necessary, add more dressing and toss until everything is lightly coated.

STEP 7: Add Croutons

If you like croutons, add them last, after the salad has been dressed and each salad has been plated. They'll start on top and won't get soggy that way.

Lettuce and Greens

Despite the crunchy stem, they have a mild flavor and are extremely pliable. Salads have an advantage from their uneven, ruffled surfaces, which add layers of texture.

Loose Leaf lettuce

Looseleaf lettuce is adaptable and useful in a number of applications. The ideal method for preparing the leaves for salad is to break them into bite-sized pieces due to their size. They make wonderful lettuce wraps.

Cabbage from Napa Valley

Napa cabbage has a milder, slightly sweeter flavor than the usual green cabbage and is a nice crispy change of pace from your regular leafy green. It's commonly used in kimchi, soups, and as a stuffing for dumplings, but napa cabbage can be eaten in a variety of ways. Try shredding it into a slaw, tossing it with noodles, or stuffing it into a filling wrap.

Romaine lettuce

This large leafy lettuce is stiffer than others, with a thick center rib that gives it a nice crunch. This lettuce has a slight bitterness due to the rib. This is the lettuce that was originally used in the Caesar salad.

When you want superior crunch from your greens or a sturdy variety that can withstand the grill, reach for romaine.

Lettuce iceberg

Crisphead, Reine de Glace, and Igloo lettuce are some of the other names for this lettuce.

Iceberg is known for being a crisp, watery, and refreshing beverage. It grows in basketball-sized heads with large pale-green leaves that are tightly packed.

Iceberg lettuce is the gold standard when it comes to a chopped salad or wedge salad. When shredded and filled into tacos, subs, and fried fish sandwiches, it adds a satisfying crisp, cool texture.

Arugula

Arugula can be eaten raw in salads with strong flavors, wilted into pasta, or blended into a pesto-like spread. Watercress, upland cress, curly cress, and land cress are some of the other names for this plant. All varieties have a peppery flavor. Watercress is sold in bundles and has a tough, fibrous stem with small green leaves. Because cress grows in sandy soil, be sure to thoroughly wash all types of cress.

Lettuce butterhead

Butter lettuce, Boston, bibb, Mignonette, and Buttercrunch lettuce are some of the other names/varieties.

Boston or bibb lettuce

Boston and Bibb's lettuces have soft leaves, making them a type of head lettuce. Butter lettuce has a smooth, butter-like texture, as the name implies. The more expensive Bibb is frequently sold in a plastic container to protect the delicate leaves.

Butter lettuce

Butter lettuce's delicate leaves are best used in delicate salads, but its broad, flexible leaves can also be used as a wrap.

Lettuce coral

Coral is a looseleaf variety that comes in bright green, deep red, or speckled colors. The leaves are sturdy and crisp, with tight, frilly curls and a mild flavor. Coral lettuce's tight curls are excellent at trapping dressing.

The crisp but tender variety also works well as lettuce for sandwiches or burgers.

Cress

Cress has a strong flavor, but it has a delicate texture. Use it to top a spring pizza, toss it into a sophisticated-but-easy side salad, or toss it into a saucy noodle dish.

Endive

Endive is a type of chicory with the following characteristics. It's a great addition to any salad because of its unique oval shape, soft, satiny texture, and slight bitterness. Its scoop-like shape makes it ideal for serving small appetizers.

Tear individual leaves from an endive head and serve on a crudité platter or fill them and serve as hors d'oeuvres on a tray. The leaves can also be eaten whole or sliced in salads.

Escarole

Batavian endive, escarole, and broad-leaved endive are some of the other names/varieties. This mildly bitter leafy green, which is a type of chicory, is large and crisp. Escarole is popular in Italian cuisine and is frequently used in soups and with beans. Escarole can be eaten in salads, raw, or cooked, especially when combined with beans in a stew.

Frisée

These yellow and green curled leaves have a slightly bitter taste, a crunchy stem, and a lot of texture. The producer shielded them from light during the growing process, resulting in their pale green, white, and yellow coloring. Escarole and frisée have a lot in common. The frilly texture of frisée is best enjoyed raw or slightly warmed through.

Lettuce "Little Gem"
Sucrine, Sugar Cos, and baby gem are some of the other names for this gem. Little Gem lettuce has the appearance of baby romaine, but it is actually a full-grown variety. The leaves are firm, crisp, and sweet.

Because of its small size, the leaves can be tossed whole into a salad. It's also great in sandwiches and wraps, and it can be cut in half and charred on the grill or chopped into quarters and served as a hors d'oeuvre.

Mâche
This salad green has a mild, slightly sweet flavor and is sometimes sold with its soil still attached. Trying to make a whole salad with a mâche base can be costly due to the small size of the leaves. Its leaves are also delicate and easily bruised, so handle them with caution. This delicate green is best used in salads for special occasions.

Mesclun
Spring mix and mixed baby lettuce are some of the other names for this lettuce. Mesclun is a loose mixture of tender baby lettuce leaves rather than a specific type of lettuce. There could be a variety of lettuce varieties in the mix, as well as baby spinach or other baby greens.

Pre-packaged mesclun mixes can be hit-or-miss, so if you want variety, pick a few different types from this list and combine them once you get home.

Oak Leaf

The leaves of this butter lettuce are shaped like those of an oak tree, hence the name. From afar, it looks similar to red leaf and green loose leaf lettuce, but closer inspection reveals differences in shape and texture: this type of lettuce has leaves that are shorter, and the tops of their leaves have a tender texture than red leaf and green leaf lettuce.

Radicchio

Red chicory, Chioggia, red leaf chicory, red Italian chicory, and Castelfranco are all names for the same plant.

This deep-red-purple vegetable, pronounced "rah-dick-ee-yo," is sold as a compact round head, as shown above, or as shaped as its relative, endive. It stands out because of its bright colors.

When eaten raw, this essential chicory is crisp and velvety, making it ideal for bitter lettuce fans. It can be eaten alone or complemented with other salad greens such as chicories or sweet lettuces. The red-purple hue turns brown when cooked, and what was once bitter becomes sweet.

Speckled lettuce

Many of the varieties on this list, such as romaine, looseleaf, and butterhead, may have a speckled pattern on their leaves. The bright coloring usually indicates that the lettuce is an heirloom or crossbreed type. These leaves should be kept whole or tear them into large pieces and toss them in a salad to highlight their distinct appearance.

Lettuce stems

The stalk of this lettuce variety is the real prize here, despite the fact that the floppy leaves are edible. The leaves, like escarole, can be bitter, but the peeled stalk has a nutty, cucumber-like flavor.

The leaves can be eaten raw or wilted into soups, just like any other lettuce variety. The stalks can be eaten raw, added to a stir-fry, grilled, or cooked in any way that asparagus or broccoli stems are prepared.

How to Make Salad Dressing

You'll need a clean, empty jam jar with a lid, excellent quality olive oil, white wine vinegar or lemon juice, salt, Dijon mustard, and runny honey.

1. Fill the jar with ingredients. Want one serving, do tablespoons. Want more? Measure 1/4 cup sizes. Use three parts olive oil and one part white wine vinegar or lemon juice as a base. The salad ingredients are coated in oil, and the acid from the vinegar or lemon cuts through the oiliness and adds zing.

2. Combine a pinch of salt, half a teaspoon of Dijon mustard, and half a teaspoon of runny honey in a small mixing bowl. If honey is unavailable, dissolve half a teaspoon of sugar in a small amount of boiling water. Cover with lid and shake it to mix ingredients.

3. Taste and adjust seasonings as needed by adding more of any of the above ingredients.

4. You can change up the ingredients to your liking. Instead of white wine vinegar or lemon, use red wine, balsamic, or cider vinegar. A pinch of oregano or a grind of black pepper can be added. Instead of Dijon, try a grainy French mustard.

5. Remember to shake the dressing well before pouring it over the salad, as the ingredients will separate, or serve it in a jug with a spoon for stirring. Any leftover dressing can be kept in the fridge for up to three months.

How To Steam Vegetables

Why steamed vegetables?

Bottom line, people either love or hate some veggies. You may prefer yours slathered in spicy seasonings and sauces to get them in your body. If you're already pro-veggie though, and want to take a step toward adulting, look at steaming. If you boil veggies, the water can actually dilute the nutrients. With steaming, this isn't an issue! Your vegetables retain more of the good stuff thanks to the minimal added water and gentle, indirect heat, as steaming preserves nutrients, texture, and flavor.

To make this recipe, you'll need a steamer basket, or a steamer pan. You can buy a steamer basket online that will work with any pan.

Step 1: Chop vegetables into even pieces.
Avoid the nightmare of some veggies being crunchy while others in the same bite are on the verge of being a puree.

Step 2: Place the steamer basket in the pot with water. Bring the water to a boil. When steaming vegetables, the first rule is to bring the water to a boil first! Don't be tempted to just toss everything into the steamer and start boiling the water. Fill the bottom of the saucepan or pot with about 1 inch of water, then place the steamer basket inside. The water should be just below the basket.

Step 3: Add vegetables. Cover and steam until desired tenderness. About 15 minutes.

Don't hesitate to adjust the time as it's more about the thickness of the cut than simply the type of veggie it is.

The most crucial aspect is taste! To determine whether a piece is done, use a fork to test it and taste it. The cooking time will differ depending on the thickness of the chopped vegetables and the maturity of the vegetable.

Step 4: Drain and season with salt and pepper.
Transfer the vegetables to a bowl with care. Then toss with kosher salt and olive oil or butter. Use lemon juice, fresh herbs, cheese crumbles, or other spices to add some pizaz to the flavor.

How Long to Steam?

Artichokes, Baby – 5- 6 mins
Asparagus– 3- 6 mins
Artichokes, Full-Size – 35-40 mins
Green Wax, Beans – 15- 18 mins
Bean Sprouts – 3 mins
Beets – 30- 35 mins
Beans, String – 3- 7 mins
Broccoli, Florets – 3- 4 mins, Spears – 5- 6 mins
Broccolini – 4- 5 mins
Brussels Sprouts– 10-12 mins
Cabbage, Quartered – 20-23 mins
Cabbage, Sliced – 8-12 mins
Carrots, Sliced (1/4" -inch thick) – 5- 7 mins
Cauliflower, Florets 4-5 mins, Head (cored) 15- 20 mins
Celery – 4-7 mins
Corn on the Cob – 10-15 mins
Fennel – 10-12 mins
Greens, Hearty (kale, chard) – 5-10 mins
Greens, Soft (spinach) – 3- 5 mins or just until wilted
Leeks – 10- 15 mins
Parsnips (1.5" -inch pieces) – 8- 10 mins
Peas, Snap – 5-6 mins
Peas, Snow – 10 mins
Potatoes, Small – 10- 15 mins
Potatoes, Sweet - 12- 15 mins
Spinach – 3- 5 mins
Squash – 30 mins
Turnips (1/4" -inch slices) – 15 mins
Winter squash– 15 to 20 mins
Zucchini (1/4" -inch slices)– 5 to 7 mins

Grocery Shopping Tips

Grocery shopping is one of the most enjoyable yet tedious chores. It can really drain you and if you're not familiar with this activity, you'll sometimes end up frustrated because of forgetting to buy something, going over budget, buying the wrong product or brand, etc.

Vital Grocery Shopping Tips

1. **Always make a list.** You are wasting money if you don't have a list. Make a list of everything you'll need, based on your weekly menu and double-check that you don't already have it in your kitchen. Plan well now so you don't forget something. Now, stick to the list.

2. **Make a weekly menu plan.** This is the most effective way to ensure that your shopping list is complete and that you have enough food to feed everyone for the entire week.

3. **Eat before you go shopping.** Otherwise, you'll end up in the Little Debbie aisle and forget all about your meal plan.

4. **Make a Budget.** You may have an unlimited budget in reality, but most people need to stay within an average, so the spending doesn't outweigh the earning. Your grocery budget is likely to grow over time, but keep a target, even if not a hard rule.

5. **Keep a running tally.** It's best to know where you're at if you want to stay within your budget, which is related to the previous tip. Keep it quick and easy if you can afford it. "$2+1+4" or "Two, three, seven, twelve," and add as you go. If your budget is tight, pull up the calculator app on your phone.

6. **Keep a list on the fridge.** Don't rely on memory when you're out of something. Some staples are assumed for each week, like milk, bread, but things like mayo need to hit the fridge list.

7. **Your Top Go-To Meals.** Keep supplies on hand for your favorite quick and easy meals. Spaghetti, chili, or macaroni and cheese, etc.

8. **Buy in bulk.** Plan to buy in bulk if you can save money. But make sure you'll use it all before it expires.

9. **Go Frozen.** It's sometimes better to buy a deep freezer for the extra space and get frozen veggies. You can shop during sales and store them for longer

times than fresh produce. You may not have quite the nutritional value, but freezing shouldn't zap too many nutrients.

10. **Leftovers!** Make a little extra for each dinner so you'll have leftovers for your lunch.

11. **Meal Prep.** Cook larger batches and then freeze it. Cooking a week's worth of dinners on one Sunday is a fantastic idea. Plan 5-6 freezer-friendly dinners and cook them all at the same time.

12. **Instant and Crock Pot dinners**. Yesterday's crock pot and today's instant pot simplify your busy life. There may be a slight learning curve but find a free group on social media and go for it! Cut up a bunch of ingredients in the morning, throw them in the pot, and dinner will be waiting when you get home.

13. **Coupons.** Coupons can be a pain. But many stores now have digital coupons you can load to your store app and redeem at checkout in one smooth scan. Why wouldn't you do it? Don't give your money to the big businesses when you may want a yummy milkshake with the savings!

14. **Store Promos.** I will actually shop at a store that often has BOGOs (Buy one, get one free) or Dollar Bins. – Note: Be careful with confusing BOGO FREE with BOGO 50% off. That's actually just a 25% discount and not quite the deal it seems.

15. **Generics.** The main time I've noticed a difference is on canned veggies. Sometimes there will be more stems included, meaning, likely lower quality control. If money is tight, it's something to consider.

16. **Eagle Eye.** Keep an eye on the totals as the checker scans items. Sometimes promo items will scan with regular pricing. Trust, but verify.

Food Safety

Expiration Dates

Expiration dates inform customers when a product is no longer safe to consume. On the other hand, the best-before date indicates that the food is no longer in perfect condition as of that date. Freshness, taste, aroma, and nutrients may decline.

The bottom line isn't that you need to know how long something will last, but that you learn how to read the labels. Let's dig into that a bit. It can seem overly complicated. In fact, it probably is.

If it's questionable and has been opened, you probably want to do a sniff test (does it smell the same as it did when you first opened it) or does it look the same (has it turned watery or moldy).

How long after the expiration date is food safe?

In most cases, you can eat food that has passed its sell-by date. Dairy products, for example, have a one-week shelf life after the sell-by date and eggs are safe for about a month after.

Manufacturers use the dates to convey when a product is at its optimum and are purely intended to indicate freshness. In other words, the food does not go bad or become unsuitable for ingestion. There may be no difference in taste or quality between refrigerated and non-refrigerated foods, and expired foods do not always make people sick.

Best Before / Use by: This is a quality assurance date that serves as a "suggestive" for when the food's flavor and quality are at their best. Make sure you read the specific wording. The date isn't the only thing to pay attention to. Learn the differences so you don't waste food

Use By: This is the recommended date for you to consume the food. However, just because it's a day or two past the use-by date doesn't mean it'll make you sick if you eat it, though you should assess the food's quality after that time. Remember, the sniff test and the visual check for mold or changes can help you make the most of your money. When in doubt, throw it out.

Sell By: If you're in the grocery store and the last unit of your favorite yogurt hasn't sold by the end of the day, you can still buy it. This isn't a safety date; rather, it's a date used by retailers to determine how long an item should be kept on the shelf. "One-third of a food's shelf-life remains after the sell-by date for the consumer to use at home," according to the IFT.

This date tells when a product should be frozen to sustain peak quality, according to the USDA. This isn't a purchase or expiration date.

Here are some important tips about food expiration:

- Refrigerated eggs should be consumed within 3 to 5 weeks.
- Yogurt should be consumed within 2 weeks if refrigerated, and within 2 months if frozen.
- Milk should be consumed within one week if refrigerated, and three months if frozen.
- When refrigerated, butter should be consumed within 3 months; when frozen, it should be consumed within 6 months.
- Refrigerated bacon should be consumed within 2 weeks if unopened or 1 week if opened; frozen bacon should be consumed within 1 month.
- Refrigerated hot dogs should be consumed within 2 weeks if unopened, or 1 week if opened; frozen hot dogs should be consumed within 1 to 2 months.
- When refrigerated, ketchup should be consumed within 6 months of opening; however, it can be stored in the pantry for over a year, if unopened.
- Mayonnaise should be consumed within 2 months of opening when refrigerated; however, it can be stored in the pantry for 3 months if unopened.
- Jams and jellies should be consumed within 6 months of opening when refrigerated; they can be stored in the pantry for a year
- Rice and dried pasta should be consumed within two years.

- Bottles and cans of beer - When refrigerated, consume within 1 day of opening: store in the pantry for up to 9 months.
- Bottles and cans of soda - When refrigerated, consume within 2 days of opening: store in the pantry for up to 6 months.

Expiration Label Reading Instructions:

- Check the use-by, sell-by, and expiration dates on the product. The sell-by, use-by, and expiration dates indicate how long a product should be kept on the shelf and provide an estimate of how long the food will taste its best.
- The month, day, and year are usually included in these dates. The date can be written out or in a traditional numeric format. After the sell-by or use-by dates, food may still be edible.
- For instance, the sell-by date could be "Sell by March 24, 2027" or "Use by March 24, 2027."
- If you come across a product that has passed its sell-by or use-by date, you should inform a store employee.
- In some cases, the company may use the Julian Calendar, which assigns a number to each day ranging from 1 to 365. That can be perplexing because we never consider this possibility. This is most commonly used on eggs, but it is also used by some canned food manufacturers.
- The numbers like "001" and "365" stand for the 1st day of January and 31st day of December, respectively.

- If you find a three-digit code with 213 on your phone, it refers to August 1st, but it's difficult to tell without a lot of counting.
- On perishable foods, look for a three-digit numeric code. Perishable foods, such as eggs and milk, have a three-digit code because they spoil in less than a year. You can safely assume that the food was produced in the same year that you purchased it.

How to Understand Expiration Dates using the Number of Digits of the Code:

4-DIGITS

Advanced Interconnections Corp. (AIC) applies a four-digit date code label to the product directly if it fits, or to the packaging if the product is too small. The first three digits of the code represent the day of the year, and the last digit represents the year.

- DDD Y DDD will range from 001 to 366 (366 days in a leap year) and Y will range from 0 to 9. (0 for 2000, 2010, 2020 for example, and 9 for 2009, 2019, 2029) (source: https://www.advanced.com/resources-tools/documentation/date-code)

Here are some examples:
- The year code for 2016 is 6 and the date code for July 20th, 2016 is 2026. July 20th is the 202nd day of the year. (If this year is a leap year.)

- 0010 is the date code for January 1, 2010, and 3650 is the date code for December 31, 2010.
- 3655 is the code for December 31, 2015.
- Because 2016 is a leap year, the code for December 31, 2016, is 3666.
- This day-of-year code is frequently referred to as a Julian Date Code, but a Julian Date is actually a continuous count of days dating back to 4713 B.C.

5-DIGITS:

To find out when the food was made, look for a 5-digit numeric code. While most foods have clearly visible manufacture and sell-by dates, some foods, such as canned food and ready-to-consume meals, may be labeled with a 5-digit code that indicates when the food was made.

Look for a string of five numbers in a row on the bottom or sides of the meal. The year is represented by the first two numbers, while the last three numbers represent the day of the year.
- For example, if the code was 11322, you'd know that the food was made on November 22nd, 2011, the 322nd day of the year.

6-DIGITS:

Another possibility is to make the closed code entirely of numbers in the standard date order, such as MMDDYY or YYMMDD. The month-day-year code is the most common six-digit code.
- The most common code found on food products is this one.

- 111418, for example, is the date of November 14, 2018.
- The label might read "181114" for November 14, 2018, if they use the year-month-date format.

7-DIGITS:

Julian Date format is a date format that uses the combination of a year and the number of days since the beginning of that year.
- The first four digits of a 7-digit Julian date represent the year, while the last three digits represent the total number of days since the beginning of that year.

9-DIGITS:

- 190322403 is an example of a lot number.
  - The year of manufacture is indicated by the first two digits (19). (2019)
  - The next two digits (03) indicate whether the product was made in March or when it was made.
  - The following two numerals (22) denote the year's day.
  - The figures (03) represent that day's product batch.
- Because lot numbers can contain long combinations, there's a high chance of human error during the recording process.

LETTERS:

Letters usually denote the month. The letter "A" stands for the month of January, and the letter "L" stands for December.

If you think they are using an abbreviation for each month, you're mistaken; they usually don't. A set of numbers will appear after the letter to indicate the day and year, though the year may appear before the letter in some cases.

- A code like "D1617," which stands for April 16, 2017, is an example.
- Other businesses use the numbers 1-9 to represent January through September, then the first letter of their name for October, November, and December.

TIPS and Tidbits: To test eggs, place them in a glass of water. A good egg sinks, while a bad egg floats.

The USDA recommends cooking or freezing meat, poultry, and fish within two days of purchase, regardless of the expiration date on the package.

Beef, pork, lamb, veal, and poultry can be frozen for up to a year, with the exception of ground meat, which should be cooked within four months of freezing. Cooking time for lean fish like cod and flounder is 6 months, while cooking time for fatty fish like salmon is 3 months.

Lunch meat should be cooked and consumed within two months of purchase.

Pest Control in the Home

Pests. That's a nice word for the bugs and rodents that sneak into your home and steal your food, leaving a trail of poo behind them. You don't want any part of having these things in your home, let alone your kitchen or bedroom.

The following are pest control tips and tricks, but one simple word sums up most of it. Cleanliness. Bugs come where they're attracted. So, avoid making your home attractive to them.

Keep the Kitchen Clean

Pests thrive in a dirty, damp environment. Keep the kitchen counters, stovetop, racks, and drawers clean to avoid attracting pests. Wipe them down with a disinfectant cleanser on a regular basis.

Keep the Bathroom Clean

Bathroom bugs are often from your tub or sink drains. Cleaning weekly should help keep them away.

Use a toilet cleaner at least once a week, clean the sink using a powerful bathroom cleanser. Make sure if you have a shower curtain, that it is replaced as needed and there is no mold buildup.

Make sure the drain is always covered and free of debris like hair and soap. These small steps will help to keep the bathroom clean and pest-free for a longer period of time.

Don't Allow Standing Water

In some areas more than others, water may accumulate and be left sitting. If you have an air conditioner that drips water, and you have a bucket under it, that water can get really nasty before someone thinks to dump it out and clean the container.

Try to avoid buckets of standing water. There are pests like mosquitoes that are attracted to stagnant water, and they sometimes carry diseases. Avoid the standing water, avoid the risk of the disease.

Don't Leave Produce Out

Fruits and vegetables that are too ripe draw flies and other insects. Fruits that are cut and ripe shouldn't be left out of the refrigerator for an extended amount of time. Although certain bugs, like fruit flies are harmless, decaying fruit can draw more dangerous pests, like house flies, ants, and cockroaches, which are hard to get rid of.

Take out the Trash

Taking out the trash is more than a term of slang. Some families are 'trashier' than others – Excuse the pun. No offense intended.

If you buy a lot of packaged groceries, you'll be filling your trash can with bulkier things like food packaging, especially if you have a lot of frozen dinners and mixes in your pantry.

That trash isn't as harmful as the trash that has food on it. If your trash has food trimmings or residue, you should ensure that the garbage is taken outside daily.

Garbage, or trash with food or stinky things in it, can attract mice and roaches. Trust me, these little beings may serve a purpose in the world, but they need to fulfill their purposes outside.

Keep Your Garden Tended
Fill in holes or pits where water can collect if you have a lawn or garden. Clean any ponds or water fountains on a regular basis. To avoid unwanted pests such as mosquitoes, rats, and ants, keep your garden neat and under control.

Keep the Outside, Outside
Just like you don't store your pajamas out in the garage, you wouldn't want to bring in your outdoor tools inside. While using a step ladder for both inside and outside may seem harmless, if you use it outside, but want it inside, make sure you hose it off first and dry it to make sure you aren't bring bugs and germy filth inside.

The same goes for outdoor toys like battery-operated cars, bicycles, and other similar items. Keep them locked up in the garage or another outdoor location. See, your mom was right about not bringing your boards and scooters inside!

Declutter

Decluttering your areas like your bedroom or if you have boxes of things in the attic, garage or crawlspace of the house all are super appealing to bugs who are looking for a way to stay warm.

Did you know that roaches love cardboard? I didn't either, until I had a pallet of cardboard boxes delivered to my new home business location. Within a week, this spotless garage was crawling with roaches. No food. Just cardboard. Needless to say, we had to call an exterminator!

Word of warning, if you're a magazine or comic collector, be sure you store your collection in a safe, dry location.

Hire a Professional

While the measures listed above can help reduce the number of pests in your home, you will need professional assistance to completely eliminate pests if you're aware of an issue. Most homes have a stray bug here or there, but they're smart enough to stay away during daylight and populated areas. If you see them, you may have an issue.

Plants to Avoid Insects

You can buy these plants and place them inside the house to naturally prevent pests and insects. Note: If you have indoor pets, do your research to make sure they're safe for your animals to be in the area.

The Right Tools Matter

Biological

Biological pest control methods, which involve the deployment of a pest's predator, are mostly used on farmland. Aphids, for example, are a pest that can destroy valuable crops and reduce harvest. Aphids' natural predators are ladybugs. As a result, releasing a stable population of ladybugs and larvae aids in the eradication of aphids while causing no harm to the crops.

The result of this method of pest control is twofold: ladybugs will proliferate if conditions are maintained. As a result, a new population will develop, and you will have a permanent control mechanism. Another advantage is that no chemicals are required, which can be costly and prohibitive for organic crops.

The effectiveness of biological pest control varies depending on the predator's ability to reproduce and adapt to the new environment. Because you're relying on the breeding cycle, it's a slower method of control. Furthermore, the predator can sometimes become the pest as well—a delicate balance.

Trapping

Traps are a common practice for outdoor pest control and, if possible, the preferred option for rodents. This is simply due to the traps' reusability and low toxicity. This is usually the best option if the problem isn't dangerous and is just annoying.

Traps assist in attracting pests to a central location and preventing them from fleeing. After being trapped, they are either relocated or exterminated.

Non-toxic adhesive traps, on the other hand, use a large sticky pad placed in a high-activity area. When pests walk on the sticky pad, they become stuck until they die. You need to determine for yourself if you view pests as something you should kill or just remove.

Glue traps can seem cruel. It's much more humane to avoid letting them into your home in the first place, so you don't have the moral dilemma of if they need to die or be removed.

First Aid from Pesticides

If You've Been Exposed to Pesticides, you should always err on the side of caution. If you can't find this book quickly, you should waste no time, but quickly search the internet for EPA.gov or poison.org. Every second matters.

If a pesticide has been swallowed, inhaled, or gotten into the eyes or on the skin:
- If the person is unconscious, has difficulty breathing, or is convulsing, dial 911 and describe what you know. Information is the most important tool medical teams have to help someone through this.
- Check the product's label for first-aid instructions.

> **For more information on first aid, call the**
> **Poison Control Center at**
> **(800) 222-1222**
> **National Pesticide Information Center (NPIC)**
> **(800) 858-7378**

What to do if:

- **Poison was consumed.** Only induce vomiting if specifically instructed to do so by emergency personnel on the phone or on the product label. It depends on what the person has swallowed; some petroleum products or caustic poisons will cause more harm if forced to vomit. If emergency personnel recommend it, keep Ipecac Syrup on hand to induce vomiting. Make sure it is not expired.

- **Poison has been injected into my eye.** If poison gets into your eye, keep your eyelid open and wash it for at least 15 minutes with clean running water from the tap or a gentle stream from a hose. While the victim is being treated, have someone else contact a Poison Control Center on your behalf.

- **Poison due to skin exposure.** If pesticide gets on your skin, wash it off with water and take off any contaminated clothing. Soap and water should be used to thoroughly cleanse the skin and hair. Later, discard the contaminated clothing or wash it separately from the rest of your laundry.

- **Poison was inhaled.** Carry or drag the victim outside as soon as possible. If you believe you require protection such as a respirator but do not have one, call 911 and wait for requested emergency equipment before entering the area.

Loosen the victim's restrictive clothing. If the victim's skin has turned blue or has stopped breathing, perform CPR if you are trained to do so and call for assistance. Open the doors and windows to ensure that no one else is poisoned by the fumes.

NOTE: Do not perform CPR if you are untrained. You may do more harm than good. Immediately call 911 for assistance and take direction from the trained emergency worker on the other end of the phone until help arrives.

Symptoms of Being Poisoned

NOTE: *If you see moderate to severe symptoms, go to the doctor immediately for checkup.*

MILD POISONING SYMPTOMS:
- Nose, throat, eyes, or skin irritation
- Headache
- Dizziness
- Decrease in appetite
- Thirst / nausea
- Diarrhea, sweating, apathy, or exhaustion
- Restlessness
- Nervousness
- Mood swings and insomnia

MODERATE POISONING SYMPTOMS:
- Vomiting
- Coughing and sometimes a feeling of constriction in the throat, as well as chest and abdominal cramps
- Vision blurring rapid pulse
- Sweating excessively
- Muscular incoordination trembling profound weakness
- Mental perplexity

SEVERE POISONING SYMPTOMS:
- Extra phlegm or mucous in the airways
- Inability to breathe small or pinpoint pupils
- The rate of breathing increased as a result of chemical burns on the skin.
- Reflexes are lost
- Unconsciousness
- Uncontrollable muscle twitching

EMOTIONAL
MANAGEMENT SKILLS

CHAPTER 2

E: EMOTIONAL MANAGEMENT SKILLS

Self-Care

When times are normal and easy-breezy, most take things like self-care for granted. There are those who are absolute fans and not only have regular maintenance to their bodies, like massages, hair, and nails, they know how to treat themselves at home too, to keep the stress levels down.

Others may not have ever thought it was helpful to have a self-care regimen, so they just keep going without until they reach a breaking point. Suddenly, they understand there's some level of self-care that's necessary for mental health as well as physical well-being.

I can tell you, as a person who first didn't see the point in self-care and eventually nearly melted down, I'm now a full-on advocate for the benefits of self-care. It doesn't have to be an organized system, but that's helpful if you're willing to make self-care a priority.

When life becomes a struggle, it's super important to take care of yourself mentally and physically. There are several things you can do at home to improve the health of your mind, body, and soul.

Establish a Routine

While always being busy is not something to strive for, it is necessary to keep a schedule or routine at home to take care of yourself.

It's important to keep it realistic and manageable. Wake up at the same time every day, move around, eat regularly, and stick to a bedtime schedule.

You may need to make some adjustments and be flexible but giving your day a routine will help you relax and feel more in control.

Set Smart Goals

You don't need to write great novel, though I can help you with it if that's what you want to do! It's a great idea to always have a list of S.M.A.R.T. goals. Don't set yourself up for failure. Make them realistic. It's more about keeping yourself on track.

Lean Toward Healthy Meals

Preparing and eating wholesome meals while you're at home is a great way to take care of yourself. Eating whole, nutritious foods will improve your mental and physical well-being.

Develop Mindfulness

Being more aware of your thoughts and actions is a great way to look after yourself. There are a variety of ways to practice mindfulness, and not all of them involve sitting in meditation for long periods of time each day.

Take Regular Breaks

Taking breaks is an important part of self-care. Whether you have schooling, work, or just get engrossed in a hobby or game all day, it's important to step away, clear your mind of what you've been focused on, and rebooting before going back to it.

Create a Peaceful Space

If you are not at ease in your surroundings, it will affect your mental health. So, at home, practice self-care by paying attention to your surroundings. Whether you have separate rooms for different activities, or if your kitchen table houses multiple purposes throughout the day, organize your space to maximize productivity and comfort.

Interact with Others

If your schedule is busy or you're unable to get some face to face time with others, you might want to text people you talk to throughout the day, or even schedule Skype or Zoom meetings with a group of friends you wouldn't ordinarily be able to get all together.

Be Generous

While it's critical to pay attention to your emotions and take care of yourself, channeling some of your energy outward can be beneficial in a variety of ways. You can practice minimal acts of kindness for others by picking up and delivering groceries for a friend or neighbor who is unable to do so, or have a meal delivered to someone special.

Dealing with Emotions

Self-Assessments

Our lives have a range of experiences. With those experiences, we often feel some sort of emotion. It could be excitement, sorrow, boredom, and anything in between.

Living your life to the fullest, you can expect to go through some strong feelings from one extreme to the other. Of course, you want to experience the great emotions like the first kiss, graduating school programs, and getting your first car. But emotions can't be controlled any better than you can control your life. Right?

Actually, you sort of do have the ability to control your life. You may not be able to control every aspect of it, but overall, you are the ultimate boss of your life and believe it or not, you also have the ability to control or regulate your emotions.

It's sometimes a bit of an art form because when life throws something at you from left field, you may feel like things are on a downhill spiral and you have no control over anything.

It's exactly those times that you dig deep though and take control over yourself and how you react to things that you didn't plan for.

If you don't maintain some level of control over your emotions, you may find yourself fighting everyone. It may start to feel like everyone is out to get you. I challenge you, in moments like these, try to see how it would look from an outside perspective. Would they see your life as something that was pig-piling on you? Or would they see it as something that you may not have figured out how to cope with yet?

Many people find the second scenario is more accurate if they're honest with themselves.

Emotions that get out of hand can lead to:

- problems in a friendship or a relationship
- having trouble relating to others
- difficulties at work or in school
- an encouragement to use drugs or alcohol to help you cope with your emotions
- outbursts can be physical or emotional

Take some time to reflect on how you currently handle your emotions and try to determine if you allow them to rout of control or if you keep a level of control over them. This will make identifying problem areas much easier.

Manage instead of Experience

You can't always decide which emotions you're willing to feel. Wouldn't that be a great, though? Say someone calls you a name at school. You may experience a full range of emotions from anger, hurt, betrayal, rage, sadness, and all within a few seconds of time.

Trust me, I am well aware of how it feels to have someone verbally attack you and how lost and out of control the wave of emotions can leave you feeling.

What do you do? That's the real question we need to ask.

Do you lash out at them in return? Do you get into a physical fight? Do you cry? Do you run off? Or do you just stand there, feeling the full wave of everything, and not sure how to react?

In times like this, there seems to be no great option. We'll talk a little bit about ways you can try to manage your emotions when faced with bad situations.

I want to start by saying that every person and every situation is different. If you truly feel unsafe, you should immediately seek shelter and find someone who can help protect you.

The world isn't always a safe place where we can know that good overcomes evil and we all have to become more aware of how to assess a dangerous situation from a dramatic one.

I'm sorry that you have moments where you need to quickly assess your environment and safety, but I'm glad there are skilled professionals who are finding better ways to keep us all safer in public settings.

For the rest of this section, we'll talk about emotions that are not at risk for immediate danger. I'll leave discussing other, more dangerous scenarios to those who are more equipped to cover those areas.

So, someone at the mall, that you know from school, just called you a name. What do you do? We've talked about how you feel the full range of emotions, but what action do you take?

Do you allow your emotions to direct your action? Or do you ignore the wave of emotions and just keep walking in a different direction?

I don't want to coach you in a direction differently than your trusted adults, but I ask you to think of these scenarios before they happen, so you'll be better able to handle them if they do pop up.

Ignoring your emotions or suppressing them isn't healthy. Acting on them without first considering possible consequences is also not a good idea.

What could be an acceptable response to that situation?

I would suggest you allow yourself to feel the emotions and determine how they make you feel. Do the emotions make you feel sad or angry?

This is the toughest part, you should try to practice thinking quickly, in spite of the overwhelming emotions that are coursing through your body, and determine the following:

1. Do they mean to harm you physically?
2. Do they mean to hurt your feelings?
3. Do they understand how their words feel on the receiving end?
4. Are they hurting or scared and lashing out badly?

If you can assess a confrontational situation with these questions, you may be better able to manage your own emotions even when others don't manage theirs.

If you are sure they have ill intentions, maybe walking away is a good solution.

If you're not sure of their intention and think they may have said something without thinking it through and you're able to manage your own emotions, you might ask a follow up question.

I know the situation may seem heated, but I can tell you, many times, I've been in conversations that were building toward a confrontation, but a simple question helped diffuse it.

In this situation, you could ask them, "Dude, I'm not sure if you're having a bad day or what, but are you okay?"

Sometimes a response like this could make them realize they really don't want to fight with you, and they're just not managing their emotions well.

On the flip side, if someone asks you if you're having a bad day, stop and ask yourself if you said something that might be hurtful to someone else.

Many conversations that end up in a fight could be avoided if the participants could just manage their emotions, and their tongue, long enough to think their way through how to deescalate things.

Not being able to manage your emotions can cause mental and physical health issues, including:

- anxiety & depression
- issues with sleep
- tension and pain in the muscles
- a problem with stress management
- Misuse of drugs

Make sure you're not just sweeping emotions under the rug when learning to control them. Finding a healthy emotional balance between overwhelming emotions and no emotions at all is essential for healthy emotional expression.

General Mental Health

In previous generations, kids and young adults didn't talk about mental health or the struggles of growing up. It's something everyone remembered being tough, but it was pretty much lumped together as part of learning to deal with life as a whole.

While that may be accurate, there has been more light shown on the fact that as the world becomes desensitized to violence and cruelty, we need to make sure everyone understands the differences between reality and fiction.

If you're a gamer, I'm certain you already know what I'm talking about. Someone should be able to play the games where there are wars or other battles that can hone your motor skills and reflexes and provide enjoyment to the player without it causing someone to believe it's acceptable to go out and kill people in real life.

Most have a very clear understanding of this. Some get it confused and take their frustrations from fictional to reality. I am not a doctor, so I can't speak to how you can know if you will be one of the people who get it confused or not, but if there's any part of your mind that begins to think or plot harm against real people, please reach out to someone for help.

Games, books, and movies with drugs, sex, and abuse may seem realistic, but make sure that even though it's something that could happen, and sadly, probably does happen out there, it's not something that should be modeled. I won't harp on this but do need to make sure you know to look for those thoughts in your own mind, so you can be the one in control of your actions.

Because of some of the horrible things that younger people have done in the past decades though, it has become evident that just because you're younger, it doesn't mean that your life is all rainbows and unicorns. Life can be tough!

One thing to point out is you should be aware of your own 'mental health' and make sure you take steps to keep yourself cared for. Your parents likely are on the job making sure you're okay as well, but just in case they don't notice when you're feeling more stressed than usual, be responsible enough to take care of yourself or reach out for help. There is zero shame in asking for help, whether it's a hug or to talk with someone about what's stressing you.

Let's explore some basic mental health tips to help you avoid falling into a negative mindset. Everyone will dip into the negative pool, but the goal is not to dive in and soak in it. Recognize any thoughts that may not be healthy and hatch a plan to rid yourself of as much negativity as possible.

Personal Connection

Calls, messages, and social media are excellent ways to stay in touch with others, but there's nothing like good old face-to-face contact. You decide how often fits into your schedule but try to have at least occasional meet ups with others, so you don't lose the ability to function socially.

Ways to Stay Connected

- Discuss your feelings with a friend
- Volunteering can help you and others
- Spend some time with a friend
- Make a phone call or send an email just to check in with friends you haven't chatted with lately
- Make a weekly dinner meetup with a parent or BFF
- Take a class or join a club to meet new people

Do Fun Things

Staying active is a great way to keep your mind focused on fun and productive things. If you spend all your time sitting at the computer or couch, your mind may start to lose focus.

You can take up a hobby, sport or learn something new like music, art, or writing to express yourself creatively. Spend time with your friends. Visit an art gallery, the mountains, or a baseball game on a day trip.

Health Matters

Shoot for eight hours of sleep each night. Learn healthy sleep habits like making sure you have a somewhat regular sleep schedule and that those eight hours are in one sleep. Naps are cool too but try to give your body time to rest and regenerate.

Avoid Stress

Stress is one of those things that many adults forget younger people also feel. If you start feeling stressed about something, make sure you share your feelings with your parent or someone you trust.

It's possible that you're putting too much pressure on yourself. Stress, if temporary, isn't entirely bad. It teaches you how to cope with uncomfortable situations and you can learn troubleshooting techniques to overcome tough scenarios.

That said, stress isn't something you should have to learn to function under on a regular basis. Some people believe they thrive on stressful situations because they've had to learn to succeed despite stressful times. Sadly, your mental and physical resources will drain if you are stressed all the time.

Sleep

We all have been told to get eight hours of sleep per night. You know you can be just fine with fewer though, so you stay up late and then you're wiped out the next morning. I get it! We all tend to do this until we realize what a toll it takes on our entire system.
You might want to set your alarm to drift off to a soft sleepy music and then have your alarm in the morning wake you up gently to a vibey energetic and positive station to wake you up on the right side of the bed.

Relax

Daily relaxation can help reduce stress and increase feelings of happiness and well-being. There will be times when you know you're feeling stressed and need to relax but may not be able to figure out how. Yoga, deep breathing, and meditation are all good options.

Yoga may seem like something only certain people do. I know I always thought that people who did yoga were strange when I was young. I didn't understand all the poses and why people did yoga.

Once I understood that it's about stretching your body and holding it in certain poses to build strength without having to lift weights, it started to make more sense. Yoga has become a great way to get exercise in on a regular basis, even if your body is in poor condition.

I also used to believe that meditation was for weirdos. I'm now one of those weirdos, because I love to take anywhere from five minutes to about thirty minutes to let my body know that I'm in control and to give my mind and body a break from the stressors of the day.

If you haven't done meditation or yoga yet, you can go to YouTube and find examples and decide for yourself. Feel free to reach out to me and let me know what you think!

Get Your Moves On

Physical activities are important for people of all ages, but at younger ages, you're establishing habits that will take you throughout your life. If you start off being lazy, the odds are that you'll stay that way.

On the other hand, if you start off being active by exercising and keeping your body moving now, you have a better shot at keeping your body in better shape longer than you may otherwise.

The estimated optimal time for activity is about 30 minutes a day, but if you're having fun, there's no need to stop there. You can do strength or cardio exercises, or a combination of all types, or you can just run, play, dance, swim, and anything else that keeps your body moving and getting stronger and healthier.

Food for Thought

Did you know that the food you put in your body had specific functions once you've eaten it? Did you know that there's so much scientific research into food and how it impacts your body, that the world knows that certain foods perform specific roles toward your health?

When I was young, all I knew was 'vegetables are good for you,' and 'too much junk is bad for you.' But the science is out there, and it's very clear that what you eat has a direct impact on your good or poor health.

It can be overwhelming to understand all the good things and bad things, even as an adult. Thankfully, many people are realizing that we, especially in the United

States, have done a pretty lousy job of caring about our health.

I challenge you to find a way to eat the good stuff and limit the foods that are considered junk-food as a positive daily habit. You may question which is which. There are many books available by pros in the nutrition field, but if you ever are curious, you can also search the internet for health tips.

There are different food plans that some families follow either from habit or their environment or due to health or medical concerns. But most tend to agree that vegetables are good for your body. Some are better than others, based on what your body needs, but currently the suggestion is to try to eat a variety of colors when it comes to veggies.

Other foods like meats and grains seem to be up for individual preference. Some suggest against one or the other while some tell us to avoid both and stick with plants/veggies.

Another thing most agree on is that sugar, while yummy, should either be avoided entirely or at least limited as it doesn't seem to have many benefits to the body other than possibly the happy feeling you get when you eat an ice cream cone.

If you and your family are trying to avoid sugars, there are some sugar substitutes that will still let you have the goodies without the health concerns. Almost anything in moderation is usually okay as far as the body goes but starting good eating habits now will very likely carry you into adulthood with a great outlook.

Soak up the Sun

Did you know that some people actually need the sunlight to avoid depression? There's a condition called Seasonal Affective Disorder (SAD) that impacts some people to the point they become depressed.

Exposure to sunlight can literally improve your mood and health. Look it up! Search "Serotonin sun dopamine" and see what pops up. I don't know about you, but when I was young, I didn't learn all these cool science-y things. You can actually learn a lot by geeking out with some research time.

When possible, make sure you get yourself outside during the day and soak in the sun for at least 15 minutes. See if your family is aware of the importance of getting outside each day and challenge everyone, even parents, to make this a daily habit!

This is another reason you should try to sleep at night and be awake during daylight hours. If you can't get outside for some reason, at least make sure you open the blinds or curtains and let the light in.

It's Never Always

Overgeneralization is one of those things that can get you mentally stuck. Making broad generalizations based on a negative experience and believing that it's always going to be the case, can get you into a funk.

If you struggle with a certain subject at school in the first week of class, you might think, "I'm no good at this!" when the truth is probably just that it's not something that has clicked yet, and when it does, you'll be great at it.

But when you tell yourself that you're not good at something, you're going to believe it because it came from you! You have the ability to train your own mind, so you want to make sure you teach it things that aren't negative. Let's say you're the shortest kid in the class and you love basketball, but at your height, just think how easy it would be to tell yourself that you'll never be able to play pro basketball.

If you told yourself that, you'd be right. How? Because you wouldn't believe it was possible, and you wouldn't try to accomplish it. If someone else told you that you'd never be able to make it, you might be determined to prove them wrong.

But you won't try to prove yourself wrong. That's why it's so important to make sure what you tell yourself doesn't limit your potential. You can do anything you set your mind to and put energy toward.

Avoiding Assumptions

Sometimes relationships with friends can become overwhelming. It may be a best friend or someone you're interested in dating or any relationship in between.

Let's say you ask someone out and they say they will have to check and will get back with you. You wait a few days, and they haven't reached back out.

Do you assume they're not interested and decide they're not worthy of you? Or do you reach out to them and check back with them?

Sometimes assumptions derail great things. This is something that may always happen. I still experience it even in my fifties! I would like to challenge you not to assume something that you have no way of knowing if it's true or not.

Now, if someone tells you no, you probably don't need to keep asking. No means no. But, if they seem interested, but don't quite say yes. Isn't the potential worth a follow up text?

Many relationships in generations before yours began by one person not being entirely thrilled at the thought of dating someone. Then, they ended up getting to know the person, fell in love, and were married until the end.

Keeping in mind, that no means no, if you get a no, accept the answer and move on. But silence could just mean that they're busy, their phone is turned to silent, or they're waiting for a parent to give permission and may not want to share that tidbit with you just yet.

Whatever situation you may be experiencing at any given time, try to assess the following:

1. What are you feeling?
2. Is it possible you're making a false assumption?
3. What's the worst case scenario?
4. What's the best case scenario?
5. Do you care enough about 'it' (whatever 'it' is in each situation), to stay calm and ask a question?

If your answers through these questions lead you to believing you don't care about it enough to follow up or ask another question, move on. There's no reason to lose energy over something that you don't actually care about in the first place.

If you do care about 'it' though, stop overthinking or making assumptions that you can't possibly know the answer to, and follow up.

Reframing Thoughts

Reframing thoughts is a term that just means that you stop yourself from thinking negative things, or making assumptions, by considering possible alternatives, which can help you modify your initial reaction.

In the case where you asked someone out and they hadn't responded yet, you may let your emotions get away from you, and assume they hate you, or they're not interested, or maybe they're even showing your text to their friends, and everyone is making fun of you. It's sometimes human nature for our minds to go to the worst case scenario. Before you know it, you're feeling that worst-case scenario.

Please avoid this the second you catch yourself thinking this way. That person may actually be doing a happy dance on their end of the phone and giggling so much, they can't type yet.

Try to reframe the way your emotions start at worst-case. The reality is probably somewhere between the two extremes, and the details are impossible to know... until you know.

So, remind yourself of other possible situations. You're your own BFF and you want to settle that insecure little voice in your head that brings the worst-case scenarios to mind.

Remember, if you care about the truth, it's worth reaching out with a follow up. Then you'll know the truth, and all the wasted energy can be avoided.

Accept Your Feelings and Emotions

Sometimes, a person is taught not to let others see you sweat or cry. There are people who view emotions as weakness. I urge you not to be extreme on emotions. The fact of the matter is that emotions are there, in your life, for a reason.

Fear is an emotion that, at least back in caveman times, helped you identify when you were in danger. Today, you may still think you feel fear about failing a test or being rejected for a club you want to join. I won't go into it now, but that isn't necessarily fear, as much as concern or worry, and we call it fear.

These emotions are in your system to help you identify potential dangers and to help you enjoy some of the amazing moments you will go through.

If you're taught to hide emotions, whether by example or being told it shows weakness, I urge you to do some research and confirm that emotions don't make you weak. They're wonderful and beautiful things.

That said, there may be moments that you may want to manage your emotions. If you get an amazing score on an entrance exam for a program you've dreamed of for years, by all means, jump up and down and scream with joy!

Now, if you open that email with your results during the middle of a wedding ceremony, yeah, you probably want to control your emotions until you get outside and both bride and groom have said their, "I do."

It's not the emotion you want to hide or eliminate, it's just a matter of knowing when an appropriate time is to let the joy or rage out.

If you got the email that said they were sorry, but you are not going to the next level for the program you always dreamed of, and you realize all your active hopes were put into that one dream, you may feel heartbroken, enraged, or just numb. You need to allow yourself to grieve for the loss of the opportunity of the dream you held onto for a time. Maybe that looks like screaming or crying into a pillow. It might mean venting to your parent, or just getting a hug and crying it out.

Your emotions are valid and should be felt and understood. I'm sorry to say, I asked my daughter to, "be strong, and not cry in front of relatives we were staying with," when we got the news that our cat died while we were away from home.

To this day, that's one of my biggest regrets, because I told her to hide her pain from people who loved her and would have understood. I just didn't want the deal with the possible judgement. I was entirely wrong, and I've apologized since then, but it's moments like those that can change the way a younger person will show their emotions.

My hope is that you never feel you have to hide your emotions, but that you can learn to manage how you show them, if and when appropriate. If you have a parent who isn't affectionate or a great communicator, maybe one of your great purposes in life can be to become a great communicator and a person in touch with your emotions in spite of not having perfect role models.

Depression

Does it seem like you feel depressed a lot?

It's a good idea to be clear on what depression is before you diagnose yourself. Psychiatry.org calls depression a common and serious medical illness that negatively affects how you feel, the way you think and how you act.

With that definition in mind, you may realize that you're not depressed as much as you may feel other emotions that come and go based on how your life is going at the time.

The Mayo Clinic writes on its website that depression is a mood disorder that causes a persistent feeling of sadness and loss of interest.

With these definitions in mind, my hope is that you don't have depression, but you should be aware of what depression is and some tips on how to avoid it, when possible.

You can absolutely feel depressed or disappointed, sad or any other emotion that is associated with depression without actually having depression.

The main difference between feeling depressed and being depressed is how long that emotion stays, and how strongly it wraps you up to the point you can't function as a happy person.

Depression is another emotion or illness that I strongly encourage you to seek a counselor, therapist, or other trusted adult to find help managing. A person like me may be fully qualified to talk about emotions and how to help manage them, but if you're actually feeling depressed longer than just a mood that comes and goes, you really should reach out for more help than this book can provide.

It's important that you recognize the signs of depression so you can determine if you should seek some help.

Signs You May Have Depression
- Being easily exhausted
- Concentration problems or a blank mind
- Irritable
- Sleep issues
- Constant, unreasonable fear and concern
- Fast heartbeat, headaches, hot flashes, sweating, stomach discomfort, and/or trouble breathing.
- Consistent feelings of sadness or worthlessness
- Changes in eating habits, either too much or too little

- Loss of enthusiasm for hobbies and pastimes
- Inability to unwind
- Anxiety attacks

Remember, we all get depressed from time to time. It's something you learn to manage like any other emotion. But if you are concerned that it may be more persistent, please reach out to someone for more help and tips on how to get through it.

Failure

Many people will go to great extent to avoid failing in order to avoid experiencing unpleasant emotions.

There are a variety of factors why you may feel like a failure.

The following are some of the factors that could play a role:
- Feeling Helpless
- Anxiety
- Depression
- Shallow Relationships
- Lack of Support from others
- Low Confidence
- Comparing Yourself to Others
- Self-Esteem Issues
- Negative Self-Talk
- Unrealistic Expectations of Yourself and Others

The main thing you need to understand with this emotion is that it's just that. It's an emotion. If we've already established that you can monitor and control emotions, this is just another thing to manage.

You should never, ever think that you are a failure! Like never!

You may fail at something you do, but that's just the thing you failed at, so far. It's not who you are. This can be confusing at first, and especially around others who may be better at some things, it's easier to believe yourself as a failure. Stop it! YOU are not a failure. You just may not be as blessed in certain areas as others, or maybe you just need some extra practice.

Accept Your Feelings

Embarrassment, anxiety, anger, sadness, and shame are just a few of the emotions that come with failure. Those feelings can suck. I get it. But feelings and emotions come and go. You don't need to invite them to stay and live with you.

If you have a competitive nature, use the fail to motivate yourself to push harder and keep trying. If it's something you must complete successfully, push, and focus until you complete it, and then let it go. Often, it's simply extra practice that's required to get better at something. You got this!

Remember, in meditation and reframing mindset exercises, you want to allow yourself to feel the emotions. Then you can choose to take an action to get better, or if it's something that has no relevance on your life, you can simply set it aside entirely and revisit it at a later time.

You may not be emotionally ready to succeed at that task yet. If that's the case, let it go. You don't need to lie to yourself and say it didn't matter if it did. Don't drown your sorrows in a gallon of ice cream or any other form of self-medication in an attempt to mask the pain. Feel it and Free it!

Coping Techniques

Calling a friend, practicing deep breathing, going for a walk, or playing with your pet are all good ways to deal with pain. However, not every coping skill works for everyone, so it's crucial to figure out what does.

If you struggle with bad habits like smoking, drinking, or overeating when you're stressed, make a list of healthier coping options.

Illogical Fears

I worked with this guy who often said, "I never fail." I'm not sure if he said that to convince himself or others. The fact of the matter is, we all will fail at times. If you create this big-bad view of what failing at something means, you will doom yourself to thinking that failing is something much worse than it is.

Can you imagine never failing? When you learned to ride a bike, did you never lose your balance and fall over? Surely you did. Unless you are still riding with training wheels. That's what happens to people who refuse to fail. They would rather live their entire life with training wheels on so that they never fall over.

You need to learn and grow, and to do that, one day, you decide, I'm taking these dang training wheels off and if I fall, I'll get back up and try it again. I can't fall every time!

Be Realistic

Reframe your thoughts if you find yourself thinking you're a lost cause or that it's pointless to keep trying. Each time you try at something, you can't help but learn and improve on some level. If you haven't succeeded yet, it's just a matter of time.

Failure is a sign that you're trying to do something difficult or new. Expect to have a learning curve as you jump into the experience.

Don't allow yourself to put so much pressure on yourself to knock every ball out of the park. You should expect to hit some foul balls and yes, even some striking out.

Own it and Move On

Accepting a level of responsibility for the failure is critical. Own it, and let it go. Don't start pointing the finger though. That's a no-win situation. Blaming other people or the scenario for failing at something will hold your growth back. You should look for the lessons in the crappy moments. Then they serve the purpose.

Think Clinically

It's vital that you think of the situation almost like a doctor would treat a disease. Identify what went wrong and then see if there's something you can do differently next time.

Loneliness

Loneliness is a basic emotion that pretty much everyone will experience at one time or another. The interesting thing is, it's very difficult to give a blanket definition to.

You can be alone, but not feel lonely. You can be with others and still feel lonely. It's evident that loneliness isn't about being with someone as much as it is an emotion that you feel for whatever reason is specific to you.

Sadly, whatever causes you to feel lonely, the feeling can be associated with depression, introversion, low social skills, and social isolation.

As strange as it may seem, a person who is lonely may actually avoid being with others because they feel lonely. Typically, the feeling that we associate with loneliness is more about not feeling a connection to someone else, causing us to feel alone, whether we are or not.

Have you ever been in class and felt like everyone else had a best friend except for you? Or even that everyone else understood what the teacher was talking about, but you felt you were the only one who didn't?

It's a feeling of isolation or a lack of connection that often causes this emotion. It may be just a slightly sad awareness that you're apart from the rest or it could be an incredible sadness that you no longer have your best friend in your life.

You may prefer to be alone rather than with others because you might lack social skills that help you learn how to create relationships. If that's the case, you probably find yourself feeling very lonely, yet not being willing to go out and get to know others.

If this describes you, as tough as it may be to get out there and get to meet and know new people, it's usually worth the effort. That's not to say that you won't meet people that you don't want to hang out with again. It's very common that getting to know others better ends up in an experience you don't want to repeat with them.

But, on the flip side, there are going to be situations where you meet someone and realize they could be your long-lost twin. They have similar likes and dislikes and over time, you'll realize you've gained a new trusted friend. You won't ever find the great friends if you don't get outside of your comfort zone and get to know others first.

Living in such a high tech world now, it's incredibly simple to exist your entire life from your bedroom. You can attend school and socialize with social media or video games, eat, and sleep. The COVID pandemic only served to prove that humans can survive without face to face contact when necessary.

Some people have anxiety that makes it even more uncomfortable to meet new people. I was one of those people when I was young. I forced myself, in great part due to having a summer job at an amusement park, to play the role of being outgoing, even though it wasn't who I was naturally.

One might think we shouldn't push ourselves to be who we aren't naturally. I would agree on some level, but also want to encourage you, if you're shy or introverted to evaluate your feelings and try to step out of your comfort zone. There's an amazing world out here for those who push beyond their fears.

Loneliness can also result from internal concerns like low self-esteem. People who lack self-confidence often believe they are unworthy of other people's attention or respect, which can lead to isolation and chronic loneliness.

It's common to feel insecure about your thoughts and feelings. A big part of the problem is comparing yourself to others. You may have heard people comparing themselves to others, I recommend you not worry about how other people do things.

Comparing yourself to others to measure differences rarely brings out the best. For some reason, you will often assume how someone else responds are right, and your way is wrong. This can be a mindset that takes you from shy and awkward to sad and lonely.

That said, finding things you have in common can be a great exercise to find people who may become lifelong friends. I won't suggest that loneliness is a choice all the time, but often, you can find ways to avoid feeling the pain or sadness that comes with feeling temporarily lonely.

Remember, loneliness is another emotion, and you're learning that you can manage your emotions rather than having them manage you.

Journaling

Do you know that when your parents were kids, and maybe even your grandparents were young too, they often had what was then called a Diary.

They would write in it, as if they were writing to a BFF.

Dear Diary-

Today, Brad said I was a Karen for telling my mom that he was smoking after school. I thought we were friends, but I knew he'd get in trouble. Maybe I should have told him he'd better not smoke at school again, or then I'd tell. I don't know. Why is life so confusing sometimes? I thought he liked me, and now he hates me. – Your BFF, Sally Sue (obviously a made up name for a made up situation)

In today's generation, with all the technical evolutions, we now have journals. The fact that people need to pour out their thoughts and emotions into something has stood the test of time.

Why journal? Honestly, because you really are your own best friend. Of course, we're blessed with having other friends, but sometimes you may be afraid to share your innermost thoughts with others. If you've ever had your trust betrayed, you probably learned to keep some of your thoughts and emotions only for yourself.

But it's not healthy to hold so many things in if you don't have a trusted friend. Journaling is helpful because you can get the thoughts out, make them clearer in your mind than they may have been before, and it's great to go back and reread what you wrote six months or a year later. The growth and maturity you experienced can motivate you to keep going.

You don't have to put rules on journaling. Pick it up daily and let whatever comes out of you, flow freely. If you don't pick it up for a week or two, but it's within sight, that's okay. Don't force yourself. But keep it handy, because there will be moments that you'll need to purge or get clarity, and your journal will be there waiting for you.

Breathing Exercises

Whether you're ridiculously happy or unable to speak, the power of a deep breath is amazing. Slowing down and focusing on your breathing won't make your emotions disappear.

Deep breathing exercises, on the other hand, can help you ground yourself and take a step back from the initial surge of emotion, as well as any extreme reaction you want to avoid.

When you start to feel your emotions are already controlling you, do the following:

- Take a deep breath in slowly from your diaphragm. Visualize your breath arising from deep within your belly button.
- Keep it in your hands. Hold your breath for exactly three counts, then slowly exhale.

Consider reciting a mantra. Some people find that repeating a mantra, such as "I am calm" or "I am relaxed," is beneficial.

Restraint

Everything, including intense emotions, has its time and place. For example, when a loved one passes away, uncontrollable sobbing is a common reaction. After being dumped, screaming into your pillow, or even punching it, may help you release some anger and tension.

On other situations, necessitate some restraint. Screaming at your boss about an unfair disciplinary action won't help, no matter how frustrated you are.

Being aware of your surroundings and the current situation can help you figure out when it's OK to express your feelings or emotions and when you should sit with them for the time being.

Space

Sometimes, getting distance from intense feelings can help you make sure you're reacting to them the right way.

This distance could be physical, just like leaving an upsetting situation. Distracting yourself, on the other hand, can help you create some mental distance.

While you don't want to completely block or avoid feelings, it's also a good idea to divert your attention until you're in a better condition to deal with them. Just make certain you return to them. Healthily distracting yourself is only a temporary solution.

Meditation

If you are already into meditating, it may be one of your go-to methods for dealing with overwhelming emotions.

Meditation can help you in becoming more aware of all of your feelings and experiences. When you meditate, you're showing and teaching yourself to sit still with your feelings, to see them without judging or trying to alter or eliminate them.

Meditation helps the development of acceptance skills. It also has other advantages, such as helping you relax and sleep better.

Our guide to various types of meditation can assist you in getting started.

Stress

Managing your emotions becomes more difficult when you're under a lot of stress. Even people who normally have good emotional control may find it difficult to do so during times of high tension and stress.

Emotions can be made more manageable by reducing stress or finding more effective ways to deal with it.

Meditation and other mindfulness practices can also assist with stress. It may not eliminate it but can make it more bearable.

Stress-Relieving Techniques:
- getting enough sleep
- making time for friends
- exercise
- spending time in nature
- hobbies and relaxation

Consult a Therapist

If your emotions are still taking control over you, it's time to seek the assistance from the professionals.

Long-term or chronic emotional dysregulation and mood swings are associated with several mental health disorders, which may include bipolar disorder and borderline personality disorder.

There may be things that cause you to have especially difficult time managing your emotions and finding happiness. It's never a bad thing to go speak to a qualified individual who will listen without judgement and help you figure out how to overcome obstacles.

A therapist can offer sympathetic, understanding support to:
- look into what's causing your emotions to be out of whack.
- addressing extreme mood swings
- Learn how to regulate strong emotions and limited emotional expression.
- Practice challenging and reframing feelings.

Negative or unwanted thoughts can be triggered by mood swings and intense emotions, leading to feelings of hopelessness or despair.

This cycle can eventually lead to unhealthy coping mechanisms such as self-harm or even suicidal thoughts. If you're considering suicide or having suicidal thoughts, talk to someone today. Many people have these thoughts. You're not alone. You're not a freak. You're just trying to figure out how to navigate a tough time. Call someone.

If you require immediate assistance, call the Substance Abuse and Mental Health Services Administration at 800-662-HELP if you're thinking about harming yourself.

The 24-hour hotline will connect you with local mental health resources.

Self-Control

Self-control is the ability to regulate and change your responses to avoid negative behaviors, increase positive ones, and achieve long-term goals. Self-control is beneficial to one's health and well-being.

People think that in order to accomplish common objectives like exercising frequently, eating healthily, not procrastinating, quitting bad habits, and conserving money, they must possess self-control.

Self-control is referred to by a variety of terms, including discipline, determination, grit, willpower, and fortitude.

Self-control has many advantages, including improved academic performance. High levels of self-control in childhood were linked to better cardiovascular, respiratory, and dental health in adulthood, as well as improved financial status, according to one long-term health study.

Putting Off Gratification

Self-control includes the ability to delay gratification, or the ability to wait for something you want. People can often control their behavior by postponing the satisfaction of their desires.

Someone who wants to go to an expensive concert, for example, might avoid spending money on weekend shopping trips. They want to have a good time, but they know that if they wait and save their money, they can go to an exciting concert instead of going to the mall.

Short-term desires are postponed in favor of long-term rewards when you delay gratification. Researchers have discovered that the ability to delay gratification is critical not only for achieving goals but also for overall happiness and success.

Self-Talk

One thing a person of any age can do is to stay in communicate with the one person who is your forever BFF. Others will come and go over time, but you'll always be there. You may as well work on getting to really know and understand yourself as soon as possible.

When you want something, you may impulsively think you have the right to it immediately. This is an impulse that each person has to work through. Those who don't often end up on the wrong side of the law.

There is nothing in this world that is beyond your reach with time and energy invested. Nothing that you're not good enough for. That said, you always need to understand that the timing of when you will get the things you desire is not always up to you.

You may like a girl, and she may not like you in the same way. That's something you have to talk with yourself about. Get to know more about her and see if she's really someone you could like a lot.

Often times, we realize people aren't who we first think they are, so we quickly change our mind. Do your research in advance of getting into that relationship.

You cannot simply insist that she like you back. You must determine a plan. You probably would want to find out what she likes, and make sure you and she have similar likes and dislikes. Then you can start to build the friendship and maybe start dating.

There's going to be many examples you can associate with this example. From as early back as you can remember, when you took someone else's toy because you wanted it. You had to learn the concept of sharing.

Later, you wanted to buy the newest game system, but you or your parents may not have had the money to spare. You can't just take it because you want it. It's times like this that you have to do the logical self-talk that walks you through what steps you may have to go through for you to get that game system.

Maybe you want to move out of your parent's house as soon as possible. You should make sure you keep sound logic as the emotions and impulses may make you want to just leave. Many teenagers run away and those who don't return home right away often find themselves in very unhappy situations.

It's extremely important that you talk to your self-BFF and make sure that you keep your focus and energy on creating an exit plan rather than just leaving without money or resources to keep yourself safe.

Honestly, your parents, as much as they love you, fully expect you to leave home too. They have a vision of how they want it to happen. That often would include learning to become increasingly independent and making decisions for yourself as you mature, eventually leading to college, marriage, or simply leaving home with a job, a car, and a plan.

The stress that grows between parents and children as the roles stretch and change can be daunting, to say the least. The younger adults often are ready to stop being treated as someone who needs to submit to their parents, and the parents often are frustrated with the fact that the day-to-day life isn't going as they planned or expected.

Both parents and kids benefit if they talk things through in their mind before they unleash their spontaneous thoughts out onto each other.

The bottom line is, both know that the younger adult will be leaving at some point. There is love that cannot be replaced between the two sides, but it's hard to remember the love when the impulses are to flee, run, or lash out.

I promise you, you're not the only one who feels these things. But try to remember that your parent(s) want you to build an amazing life out in that big world. They're not perfect, and they're just doing their best as well. Try to focus on the goal and the plan and understand that impulsive actions and reactions will usually not turn out in the grand way you envision.

Depletion

Self-control is a finite resource, according to research. Exercising self-control over time tends to strengthen it. Self-control can be improved over time by practicing it. Self-control is, however, limited in the short term.

Concentrating all your self-control on a single goal makes it more difficult to maintain it on subsequent tasks throughout the day.

Ego depletion is a term used by psychologists to describe this phenomenon. This occurs when people exhaust their energy on one task, leaving them unable to maintain self-control for the next.

An example could be that you make yourself wake up and get ready for school after staying up way too late the night before. Now you're tired and getting cranky, but you showed up.

Then, you're faced with focusing on studying for a test that is about to start. You just don't have enough energy to care anymore. Finding a way to balance your energy is another important life skill.

Self-Control Has Health Benefits

Maintaining healthy behaviors requires self-control as well. Breakfast choices, exercise frequency, and sleep schedule consistency are all decisions that can be influenced by your level of self-control and have the potential to affect your health.

Trust me, when your parents were younger, they wanted to do all the fun things and not have to do chores like you may want. I don't know a single adult who wanted to stop having fun and work two jobs to pay the bills as a life goal.

Gradually, we learned that choices that are made have consequences, both good and bad, and if we don't want to deal with the negative consequences, it's time to start making different choices.

Things like social skills, learning responsibility and following the rules are all things that are learned. If you try to do only the things you want to do, you will fail to learn these vital learned behaviors.

Basic grooming and chores are learned skills that literally no one wanted to do for the rest of their lives. No one woke up and thought, "Yes! I get to take a shower, brush my teeth, and clean all the crap out of my bedroom before I can do anything else!" But it became a negotiation between parent to child, and then an accepted process of 'work first, then play' took over.

If you find you have no self-control, just know this is something you can improve, and it will make your life so much simpler without the strife or battles—whether internal or with others.

Suggestions for Improving Self-Control

Some suggest that self-control has its limitations and may not be able to control their own actions. For most, there are ways to manage and control the boundaries.

Some people may have impulse control issues where when they think something, they spontaneously act on it. Think about someone who steals as an example.

Some may argue that they're just wired differently than everyone else, and they can't help but act on their emotions. The reality is there may be a small population who truly and literally have no control at the time they take a negative action.

That said, the vast majority recognizes the consequences of taking actions that are not allowed, and they understand that you'll have to face that consequence if you try to steal something.

Temptation should be avoided

This is a good way to make the most of the self-control you have. By avoiding temptation, you can ensure that your available self-control is not depleted before it is truly needed.

Finding a healthy distraction can help you avoid temptation, whether it's the desire to eat, drink, spend, or engage in some other undesirable behavior.

Take a walk, call a friend, do a load of laundry, or whatever it takes to divert your attention away from whatever is tempting you right now.

Prepare ahead of time

Consider what situations might cause you to lose your resolve. What steps will you take to avoid succumbing to temptation if you are faced with it? Even in situations where people have experienced the effects of depletion, research has found that planning can improve willpower.

Self-Control is a skill that can be learned

While your willpower may be depleted in the short term, engaging in behaviors that require self-control regularly will improve your willpower over time.

The practice of meditation is a great approach to increase self-control. Being more self-aware can help you resist temptations more efficiently, so if you're new to meditation, mindfulness meditation is a great step to begin. This method can help you pause your thinking, which will help you manage any instinctual reactions that are impairing your self-control.

Remind Yourself of the Implications

Lack of self-control can harm your self-esteem, education, career, finances, relationships, and overall health and well-being, just as it can help you achieve your goals and improve your physical and mental health. Keeping these consequences in mind can help you stay motivated as you work to improve your self-control.

Spirituality

Spirituality is a broad concept that refers to a belief in something other than oneself. It can refer to religious practices that emphasize the existence of a higher force, as well as to a more general conviction of one's interconnectedness with others and the rest of the universe.

I don't want to dig too deep into this because each of us have the human right to believe what we choose to believe, and I refuse to try to coax anyone to believe what I choose simply because I'm in front of a keyboard.

I do believe it's important to evaluate what you've been told, add your own research, search your heart, mind, body, and spirit, and come to your own conclusions.

One big suggestion is that you don't judge an entire belief or group of believers by the outrageous actions of some of them. Based on your age and how much you watch the news, this will mean more to you, or less. Just know that each person you are exposed to is an individual and they should be loved or avoided as a single person, not by their beliefs.

Spirituality offers a way of looking at life that implies there is more to it than what humans can perceive. It implies that something greater connects all beings and to the universe as a whole. It also proposes that there is some sort of existence after death of our time here and often tries to provide answers to questions about the meaning of life, what makes people become connected, universal truths, and other mysteries.

Many people have found spirituality and religious activity to be a source of comfort and stress relief. Research has revealed that individuals who are more religious or spiritual and utilize their spirituality to cope with life's obstacles gain multiple health and wellbeing advantages.

Spirituality Signs

Spirituality isn't limited to a single path or set of beliefs. Spirituality and the advantages of a spiritual journey can be experienced in plenty of ways. For some, this may entail faith in a higher power or adherence to a specific religious practice.

Others could perceive a connection to a higher power or a sense of interconnection with nature and the rest of humanity. Numerous methods exist for spirituality to present itself, including:

- Developing stronger bonds with others
- Experiencing empathy and compassion for others
- Feeling a sense of interconnectedness
- Beyond material possessions and other external rewards
- In search of meaning and purpose
- The need to make the world a better place

Spirituality is not experienced or conveyed in the same way by everyone. While some look for spiritual experiences in every element of their lives, others are more prone to sense them in certain situations. It stands to reason that people want to congregate with others with similar belief systems, so you will find many join each other in churches, temples or even out in nature.

Spirituality Types

There are many types of faith or spiritual based belief systems. Again, please respect any beliefs that you don't understand as it is a personal choice. Some countries are predominantly certain types because that's what people are exposed to. It's important to do your own research and see how that sits with your own spirit.

- Buddhism
- Christianity
- Hinduism
- Humanism
- Islam
- Judaism
- New Age Spiritualism
- Sikhism
- Wicca
- Atheism
- Taoism
- Baha'i
- Confucianism
- Jainism
- Shinto
- Zoroastrianism
- Paganism

There may be others. Some of these, I hadn't heard of, so these aren't all commonly known. If you choose to do your own research, I wanted to try to provide the fullest list I could.

The Why

There are a lot of reasons why people wanted to find spiritual guidance, including but not limited to:

- To discover meaning and purpose: Spirituality can help people find answers to philosophical questions like "what is the meaning of life?" and "what purpose or reason does my life serve?" by exploring spirituality.
- To deal with stress, depression, and anxiety: Spiritual experiences can be beneficial in dealing with life's stresses.
- To restore hope and optimism: Spirituality can aid in the development of a more positive outlook on life.
- To find a sense of belonging and support: Spiritual traditions frequently involve organized religions or groups, so joining one can be a valuable source of social support.
- Spirituality's Influence

One thing to remember, if you don't have any belief of your own yet, is that people are built to have relationships with others. We want to find others who are similar to us. They say that your vibe attracts your tribe. This is very true.

When we find members of *our tribe*, we feel safer and united by something that is bigger than we are alone. Another word, not related to religion or spirituality is synergy. It's the concept that when one person collaborates with another person, they create a stronger energy together than either of them could do alone. Even if you don't believe in faiths, understand the core benefit of synergy and try to respect those who life in faith.

Religion and spirituality also can help people cope with the effects of everyday stress.

People who are at ease and at ease with using spirituality as a stress-coping mechanism can rest assured that there is more evidence that this is a good idea for them. Prayer can be effective for both young and old. It can also help with:

- Better health has been linked to prayer and spirituality
- A better mental state of mind
- Less stress during difficult times
- More feelings of happiness

Whether you're seeking a new spiritual route, reaffirming your devotion to an old one, or rediscovering a forgotten spiritual path, exploring your spiritual side may make you feel better. Each person's spiritual path is likely to be unique because spirituality is such a highly personal experience.

Notice Your Feelings Part of embracing spirituality means also embracing what it means to be human, both the good and the bad.

Focus on Others Sometimes when you take your focus off your own issues, and focus on helping others, you realize your own issues aren't as bad as you previously thought, and you feel happy for being able to impact someone else in a positive way.

Meditate There are several types of meditation. You can do some research and find several videos on platforms like YouTube where you can access some examples. The most important aspect of meditating for most is that it allows you to sit, in a calm and stress free space for a few moments a day. You can become aware of what thoughts come to your mind and recognize what may be stressing you out. Recognize and release.

Gratitude Begin a gratitude journal and write down what you are thankful for every day. This can serve as a helpful reminder of what matters most to you and brings you the most joy.

It's the simple practice of recognizing things that you are blessed by that will help you build a strong mental mindset that helps you with relationships with yourself and others. By encouraging you to be less critical of yourself and other people, being mindful can help you to focus more on the here and now rather than the past or the future.

Pitfalls to Avoid

Spiritual bypassing is one of the actual pitfalls of spirituality.

It's super important that you don't take a harsh approach to something that hurts someone. For example, say your best friend's girlfriend dumps him.

He's probably hurting pretty badly, and you may not know what to say to help him through it. Try not to gloss over it by saying something like, 'It just wasn't meant to be." Maybe you could simply ask if they want to talk about it, or ask them how that makes them feel, or if they'd like to hang out soon.

Life Lessons

What does "learn from your mistakes" mean? To figure out where and what happened, then pinpoint what went wrong, and how to make sure it doesn't happen again. By following this super basic process, you can learn life lessons.

What's a life lesson? It's a scenario where you may have to make a decision or choice, so you do, but afterward, you don't like the outcome. This could be deciding if you're going to tell your friend that someone was talking about her behind her back. If you tell her, she may be hurt or react badly, but if you don't tell her, you may feel like you're betraying her by not being fully honest about what you know.

Let's say you decide to tell her, and she confronts the person, who was also a friendly acquaintance. Your two friends now are not speaking to each other, and both may feel betrayed or sad.

This was clearly a no-win situation for you to be in the middle of, but sometimes that happens. Had you not told your friend, she would have stayed happy, but would have believed someone was a friend, who wasn't behaving like a friend.

Now that you did tell her, she trusts you more, but your other friend doesn't trust you at all. How do you learn a life lesson there? One could suggest that you don't tell the friend if they're not good friends with the person who was talking about your friend. Sometimes, it's better to let things go and just ignore them. Other times, you should absolutely speak up, especially if someone's health or safety is at risk.

Over the years, you will learn which things you should probably speak up about and which things to bite your tongue. It does get easier, but you may never master the skill.

Mistakes are often thought as something you should be ashamed of doing. But let's be clear, similar to failure, making mistakes is something that you can learn from. In fact, the hope is that you continually make smaller mistakes and learn from small consequences so that you can avoid some of the bigger ones.

Accept Responsibility

It's important to acknowledge your mistakes. So, take a deep breath and admit to yourself that you made a mistake, and then take responsibility for it. Tell those who need to be informed, apologize, and let them know that you recognize what you did wasn't the best option and that you've learned the lesson.

This simple process may be tough to perform, but if you can master this early on in life, you may find you can build solid friendships and relationships in general, that last a lifetime.

One thing that you really need to be aware of is there's a balance between accepting responsibility for your own actions and owning what isn't yours to own.

Occasionally, you may decide to take ownership of a mishap that could have been a mutual error in judgement. Maybe you and a friend stayed out past curfew, and they got in a lot more trouble than you did. You might tell their parents that you're responsible for being late to try to help your friend out.

This can be helpful to your friend and might even help reduce the sentence imposed by the parents. That said, if your friend doesn't appreciate it or if they begin to expect you to cover for their own poor choices, you should make sure you don't take ownership of someone else's bad decisions.

Additionally, sometimes when you make a series of bad choices, you may get so used to being scolded, that you either accept that you're a screw-up or choose to ignore the scolding. Neither of these are ideal scenarios.

If you've had a run of bad choices, and you're catching a lot of grief about it, you have the ability to make things right. If your parents are always telling you that you're not doing the right things, and you know you're not following the rules set for you, you can decide to get with the program and follow the rules out of respect for your parents.

On the other hand, you can ignore them and keep making the same choices you're making and wait for the consequences to get bad enough that you either have to move out of your parent's home or you live out your years at home fighting and living in a place with a negative vibe all the time.

Your parents have the right to expect you to follow the rules they create for their home. As much as you may hate it, if you're not paying the bills yet, you're still expected to be part of the family they created. The day will come when you pay the bills to your own home, and if you have others living there with you, even if you created them, you'll expect the same respect from them.

It's important to make a distinction between respecting others and treating them with respect. There will undoubtedly be times when you don't respect your parents or others.

You may feel their actions or decisions are unfair or unethical even. Be aware that even when you don't feel respect for them, you should always treat them with respect.

Sometimes, you have to accept that people who have authority over your life aren't perfect. Maybe they're just barely hanging on at times, and they may lash out at you. Try to remember that they're just people too and doing their best.

If you can try to understand their perspective, you may be able to understand a little better what they may be trying to manage at their level.

This being said, if they are abusive to you, that's not something you should have to tolerate. If you find yourself in a situation where you're not safe, please reach out to an adult, like a teacher, counselor, or other trusted adult.

It may feel scary or wrong, but you reporting abuse is likely exactly what needs to happen, and they may be able to get some help. Remember, someone probably got you this book because they wish someone had taught them how to navigate life as well. None of us are perfect, and sometimes we all need some help.

Understanding Abuse

My hope is that you never have to face abuse in your life. Unfortunately, abusive behavior is all too common in the world today.

- The CDC website reports that at least 1 in 7 children have experienced child abuse or neglect in the past year.

- A report by the RAND Corporation states that as many as 13.1% of men and 12.4% of women experience verbal abuse regularly at work.

- In the United States, VeryWellHealth.com indicates that 1 in 3 women and 1 in 4 men have experienced some form of sexual abuse through rape, physical violence, or stalking.

These are just some numbers I found doing a quick internet search. Honestly, I hate to dig too deep into this because it can be scary and a bit depressing that so many people are being treated like this.

There are many forms of abuse, and we'll share some of the primary types so you can make sure to recognize it if you or someone you care about has been exposed to these abusive relationships.

A pattern of attitude in which one person dominates and controls another is known as domestic violence. This is most common among intimate partners. Abuse of any kind, whether it be physical, psychological, emotional, verbal, sexual, or financially, is used to assert authority and control.

When people think of "abuse," most of them immediately think of physical violence, but domestic violence can be much more than that. It frequently includes a wide range of controlling behaviors.

Types of Abuse

Physical Abuse
Hitting or slapping, kicking, choking, pushing, and punching.

Verbal Harassment
Criticism or mockery, humiliating remarks, yelling, swearing, or calling people names.

Sexual Harassment
Forcing you to have sexual intercourse, demanding sexual acts, taking sexual photographs without your permission.

Isolation
Controlling activities, taking car keys, destroying passport, monitoring phone calls, reading mail, texts, or making it difficult to see friends and relatives.

Intimidation
Creating or causing guilt, fear, or shame, manipulating children, insisting on being right.

Stalking

Sometimes a person becomes obsessed and starts to track the moments of someone else. They may monitor social media, send gifts, or even break into your home. While this may feel flattering at first, it quickly can get out of control, so be aware of the risks and signs.

Economic Control

Refusing to pay bills that you need paid to keep a roof over your head or allow you to go to school or work.

Threats and Intimidation

Threats to harm children, other family members, friends, or coworkers, or pets to hold control over you. Intimidation through size, threatening bodily harm.

Emotional Withholding

When abuser is cold and without emotion, they show no love or care for the person they have a relationship.

Destroying Property

Abuser will punch holes into walls or throw to scare.

Self-Destructive Behaviors

Abusing drugs or alcohol, threatening self-harm or suicide, or driving while intoxicated or reckless. While these are self-harming, the person who loves them is also hurting from it.

Is a Friend Being Abused

If you have a suspicion a friend or family member is being abused, speak with them privately to express your concerns, and offer assistance. Here are some suggestions:

- Find a quiet, private space where you can talk without being distracted.
- Express your concerns and ask if your suspicions are correct.
- Even if you can't relate to their situation, show that you care about and empathize with the person.
- Do not exert pressure, pass judgment, or attempt to exert control over the situation. Offer resources where they can get help if they're not yet ready to get out of the situation. Often, the victim truly loves the abuser and hopes that the situation will change. It rarely does.
- Check back with them again, especially if you see new signs that the abuse has continued. They may be afraid to admit they were wrong in holding out hope.

Losing a Parent or Close Relative

The pain of losing a parent or close relative is potentially the worst thing you may have to face in your life. Your parent starts out as your caregiver and the one person who has your back no matter what.

Over the years, you may change the way you think about them. Things may be less than ideal, but no matter how much they nag to get you to do your chores and schoolwork, I bet, deep down, you still know they love you more than anything in the world.

There's something that changes in a person when they have a baby. They stop thinking only of themselves. That child... you, become the center of their entire world.

As you grow up and become more self-sufficient, your parent may start to migrate back to finding things that make them happy again. They may have a career they love instead of a job they're simply forced to do to survive. Sometimes their focus on work may make you feel like they are less concerned with your life and happiness, but I promise you, it's not the case.

The reality of life is that parents recognize that one day, you're going to grow up and leave them, and they need to be able to survive, and hopefully thrive in their own lives once you've moved out.

They understand that a parent's job is to raise you to learn how to survive on your own, and they want to help you find your own happiness and path that will make you happy.

The whole circle of life thing is part of life, whether we like it or not. Our best hope is that we live each day, sharing love and happy moments with our family and friends, and when it's time to say goodbye, we have left enough good memories behind for those who are still here.

When you face the loss of a loved relative, it may happen at any time. You may or may not have known to expect it. Often, kiddos aren't told about some things, because parents are trying to protect you from worrying about things that you can't change the outcome on.

If you lose someone to a disease, please don't be angry that you weren't told in advance. They made a decision to try to help you experience as little pain as possible with the reality that was impending.

When you're a little bit older, the adults may share with you the information and let you have focus time with the person who is ill. Even if you aren't aware of it yet, those moments you are able to spend with them will become memories that you will hold onto forever. Try to spend time smiling and laughing with them, rather than focusing on the fears and pain.

That said, it can be very healthy to be able to communicate openly about your fears about what is going to happen. If you're at an age where you can communicate openly, try to have that conversation.

Often, it's just as tough for them as it is for you. Be sensitive to their feelings as well, and make sure they know that you love them.

If they pass away and it was unexpected, the emotions you may experience are very broad and every single thing you feel is absolutely valid.

There are books that really dig deep on getting through grief that are written by people who are much more qualified than I am. I would encourage you to talk to someone about your emotions and read a book or two.

Ultimately, you need to understand that no one knows when their time will expire. No one leaves you on purpose or to hurt you. It's one of the toughest parts of life to get through. It is a process, and it will not happen overnight.

We'll cover some things to think about and suggestions, but please understand that whatever you feel at the time, whether it's numbness, anger, sadness, acceptance, or even happiness or a feeling of freedom, you should recognize the emotions and know that they will level off over time.

You can and will get through this. Be gentle with yourself and know that there will be better days ahead.

When I lost my dad, I was an adult with kiddos of my own. It still struck me with so much pain that it consumed my thoughts for a while. I had to keep functioning for my kids and my own sake, but over a decade later, when I think of my dad, I still feel a bit of pain in my heart, but mostly I remember his goofy jokes and how he'd sing his made up songs.

Make good memories today so you have something great to hold onto later.

Keep the following suggestions in mind:

- Make sure you get enough rest
- Even if you're not hungry, eat some sort of healthy snacks or small meals
- Make sure to drink plenty of water
- A daily walk can keep your body moving
- It's understandable that you might want to numb your pain with alcohol, but excessive drinking can have negative health consequences
- Reading, art, or music are all positive ways to relax
- Process your emotions by meditating or keeping a grief journal
- Seek help from friends and other family members

Talk about your Memories

Sharing stories and talking with family members and other loved ones about the person you lost can help keep their memory alive.

If you have children, you may want to tell them stories about their grandparents or continue family traditions that were important to you when you were a child.

Reminiscing may be painful at first, but as the stories flow, you may find that your grief begins to fade. Shedding a tear and laughing at the same time will become a new normal, and that's a good thing.

If you are unable to talk about it right now, gathering pictures from memorable events or sending them a letter expressing your sadness over their passing might be helpful.

Not everyone has fond memories of their parents. People also tend to keep negative memories of people who have passed away to themselves. If they abused, abandoned, or hurt you in any way, you might wonder if it's worth it to bring it up again.

If you don't want to talk about it with others close to you, at least let it process through your own mind, so it doesn't hold you back. If you can forgive them for the things that did that hurt you or held you back, you can finally gain true freedom once you no longer blame them for their bad choices.

The loss of a parent or other loved one is not easy. You may or may not be able to manage the emotions on your own. It is absolutely fine, and quite normal, for you to visit with a therapist to work your way through some of the emotions you go through at a time like this.

If no one offers this to you, take it upon yourself to find and set an appointment. Talking with a school counselor can be your first step.

LIFE
& PRACTICAL SKILLS

CHAPTER 3

L: LIFE & PRACTICAL SKILLS

Navigating through life, you'll find there are things outside the home that you may not be ready for. In the first section, we covered mostly things that you'll need to know inside your home. Section two, we covered how to manage your emotions wherever you are. Now, we're going to step outside the front door and figure out the other questions that you may face.

Cell Phones

Depending on your age, you may or may not have a phone. That phone, when you get one, quickly becomes as important to you as an arm or a leg is. At least it may seem so.

It connects you to safety by being able to dial 9-1-1 in an emergency, it is the line to communicate to your family, friends, and the whole rest of the world, and it holds so many apps that you may never look away from it!

Your cell phone is a powerful resource, but also it can become a dangerous distraction. You need to make not to walk at the same time you use it, as you could run into something. Worse, something could run into you.

There have been many accidents that occurred because someone was distracted with their phone. Please don't become part of that statistic. Always focus on one task at a time.

One of the great things about having a modern phone in your hand all the time is the vast tools at your disposal. You have the obvious, a phone and flashlight. You also have a calculator, note pad, camera, clock, calendar and maybe you're even reading this book as a digital eBook on a reader.

Then comes the fun parts, there's text messaging, social media platforms, games, movie streaming, health and fitness apps, shopping apps, banking and bill pay and of course, navigation apps.

The cell phone has become something that seems to have taken the place of friendships, relationships, and altered the way most of the world interacts with one another. I can't say if that's good or bad and I certainly can't judge, because my phone and tablet go with me everywhere.

The convenience alone is a lifesaver, but the resource a phone brings through the apps, if you use it with positive intentions, can put the world of knowledge at your fingertips at any given time.

Where people used to guess at a trivia question that pops up in conversation, now several friends will race to see who can confirm the answer on their phone through a web browser before the others.

Not sure how to spell a word? Look it up. Not sure if it's PRINCIPLE or PRINCIPAL, look it up. Your phone can level the playing field and be a huge educational resource as well as a social access point and a small-screen TV or game console. How you use it is ultimately up to you. I hope you use it for all things that bring brilliance and joy!

One word of warning. You may be fully aware already, but these tiny phones, though they're small in size, are not small in price. Please always treat it with respect regardless of who paid for it, or is making payments on it, it's easy to break a phone and pricey to repair or replace.

Use a protective cover and screen protector at all times, and make sure you have a safe place for it so you don't accidentally sit on it or drop it.

Navigation

One of the vital apps that your phone has available is navigation apps. There are many out there, and while they all have differences, they're all essentially the same. You put in your destination address and it will give you directions that you can walk, drive, or ride a bus.

Typically, the app will recognize your current location and calculate the distance, route, and time it should take to get you to the destination.

I've used these GPS apps to walk in a downtown setting, even within a mall, to find a specific store. Most of the time, I use it for daily driving. Even when I know how to get from work to home, I often use the GPS because if there is heavy traffic, the app will reroute me to a shorter option.

You can also, with some phones, share your location with others in your circle, so you can walk to each other if you're separated while out.

One thing to keep in mind, in a time when we rely so heavily on the phones and navigation, is sometimes the signal is too weak to function. Your battery may die or the phone may get damaged.

Try to make sure you have enough directional understanding of where you are and how to get to your destination should something go wrong. It's always smart to have a backup plan—and a charging cable for the vehicle and a power outlet both.

Safe Driving

Nice and Easy

Although it may be hard to resist the urge to slam on the gas as soon as the light turns green, self-control is crucial. When you gradually increase your speed, your engine operates more efficiently. Slowly escalate with gradual increase in speed until you are comfortable and keeping time with traffic or you have hit the limit.

Both Hands on the Wheel

Remember the strength of the vehicle and the power that is in your hands, literally. A quick reaction to a surprise can be exactly the perfect thing you need, or it can be disastrous.

Try to keep firm, but not clenched hands on the steering wheel as you get to know the range of motion required for the movement of the car. If your vehicle is older, you may not have power steering. That would mean you'd have more effort involved in turning the wheel than most modern day cars. Assume it's power steering if you're not sure. It's better to give not enough strength than too much to a turn.

Practice in open areas like empty parking lots until you understand where the buttons, knobs, and levers are for each tool in a car. Not knowing where your wiper blades are is a potentially dangerous thing to learn when the rain start pouring down.

Hit the Brakes

One of the most common errors when learning to drive is you hit the brakes too hard. Like power steering, most cars have power brakes.

Now, I will say that hitting the brakes too hard is probably better than not hard enough, but you greatly increase your chances of someone behind you running into you. If you don't apply enough brake, you could bump into someone in front of you.

It's no wonder driving can be intimidating. So many things can go wrong. But, as long as you take it slow and practice in safer areas first, you won't need to obsess about these things because you'll learn them in safer scenarios first.

When you apply pressure to the brake foot pad, tap it softly and then gradually add pressure until you get a feel for how it reacts. As long as you're in an empty parking lot, you'll have the space to learn these things safely.

55 Saves Lives

In many places the standard speed limit is still 55 miles per hour (MPH). However, on interstates or more populated areas, you'll see upward of 85 or as low as 15 as the speed limit.

These limits are created specifically for the areas they're posted, so if you see something that says 30 MPH as the limit, pay attention to that. There's a reason for the limit created.

If there's nothing posted, you can usually assume it's somewhere between 40-55 MPH, but typically there will be a sign somewhere. Your GPS may also let you know the speed limit if you aren't seeing the signs on the side of the roads.

Tailgaters Keep Back

Do your best to avoid tailgating others. If this is a new term, it's basically following dangerously close to the car in front of you. The word derives from your front bumper being very close to their rear bumper, or tailgate.

You may feel that you're a good enough driver to be safe very close to the car in front of you. The only problem is you don't know what type of driver they are. If they unexpectedly slam on their brakes, you're going through the rear of their car. There's zero space to allow yourself time to react.

The suggested distance between the front of your car and the rear of the car ahead of you is usually described in 'car lengths.' The number of car lengths between you and the car in front will vary based on the speed you're traveling.

The size of a vehicle and the speed it's traveling will have impact on how long it takes it to come to a stop to avoid a fender bender or wreck.

There are some who suggest you keep three seconds between vehicles. Others suggest about one car length per 10 MPH you're traveling. So, if you're on the interstate and driving at 65 MPH, you should have about 100' between vehicles.

65MPH →6.5, average car length→ 15'. *6.5x15=97.5'* suggested distance on average at 65 MPH

Lane Changes

If you're in a local area you may have one lane per direction, usually called two-way traffic. This is a basic scenario where you have your lane, and they have their lane. You stay out of each other's lane for the most part.

If you find someone in front of you is going very slowly, and you can go around them safely, you can consider passing them only if there is passing permitted in that stretch of road.

Passing is allowed when there is a dotted line in the middle between the two lanes. There are two lines in the middle, one is yours and the other is theirs. Your line, obviously, is the one closest to you.

If your line is dotted, that indicates you should be able to pass as long as you don't see any oncoming traffic. If both sides can pass freely, the two lines in the middle of the road will become a single dotted line.

Passing is one of the most common causes for very bad accidents, even fatalities. Please only pass if you are comfortable doing so and have the ability to get back in your lane quickly. It's much better to stay behind a slowpoke than end up in the ER.

Communication on the Road

You may not realize it at first, but just like people without the ability to hear can communicate with sign language, drivers have learned to communicate with other drivers.

Okay, some drivers communicate in some not-so-proper ways, but over the generations, vehicles learned to notify other drivers of intentions of turning and passing by using hand signals, horns, or flashing headlights.

Today, almost all cars have turn signals built into the cars as well as the ability to use hazard lights to notify of emergency status, and so forth. The problem is now, many people fail to use them to communicate, which often risks and sometimes causes accidents.

Your responsible to know how to communicate with other drivers and to consistently use the tools at your disposal, to be a responsible driver.

Distracted Driving

One of the main things that causes accidents in today's world is being in control of a vehicle that has extreme power to do damage, but not respecting the machine's potential.

In previous generations, it may have been trying to tune the radio dial as your parents or grandparents drove down the road. When they looked up, they may have narrowly escaped a collision. As technology improved, cars became safer from distractions.

You can adjust volume, stations and even text by voice through most vehicles today. For some reason, likely habit, many people still insist on picking up the phone and trying to text back. Please be very clear that this is not only dangerous, but it's against the law in many states to have a phone in your hand while operating the vehicle. Just don't do it.

Under the Influence

I'm sure you are aware, but I can't write about the importance of using a blinker and not clearly warn you that driving under the influence of anything that could alter your mental state is also illegal.

It can be anything from being high from weed, drunk from alcohol, or any other form of drugs or natural products that will cause you not to be able to react and think at peak performance level.

Being caught under the influence while driving can totally derail your future. At best, you don't hurt anyone, but the legal fees and blemish to your reputation and your driver's license can take years to get passed and probably cost you and/or your parents $10,000 in associated costs.

It's a big, big deal. Don't make the error in judgement.

Traffic Lights

There are many versions of traffic lights. The most common are those with red, yellow, and green circles or arrows on them. When you get to a traffic light, you should be able to see the brighter color from a distance. This helps you react early so you can avoid bumping into other vehicles.

Red: STOP
Yellow: CAUTION
Green: PROCEED cautiously

Technically, the green usually just means 'go' but I specify proceed cautiously simply because it's important that you don't blindly trust others are following the rules and paying attention.

It's not uncommon for someone to run their red light and enter into your green light, causing an accident. Just look both ways for oncoming traffic, just in case. No need to slow down unless you see something that grabs your attention in a bad way.

When you get to an intersection, you will probably see multiple lights over the intersection and wonder why so many. Sometimes they do this because your view may be blinded by other vehicles in front of you. Usually, though, there is one set of lights for each lane. So, if in doubt, verify which lane you're in and look only at the light straight ahead in your own lane.

Other traffic lights will have more than the three circles. Some will have four or more, where some will indicate a left turn or right turn arrow on the same light. This can be complicated at first, so just make sure you're looking at the correct light for the lane of traffic that you're in.

Road Signs

There are so many street signs that you'll see; you're sure to be a bit overwhelmed at first. Don't let it stress you out. Most have images that help you figure out what they mean, even if you haven't seen them before.

MOST COMMON ROAD & TRAFFIC SIGNS

Stop	Yield	All Way (Stop at intersection before proceeding)	No Left Turn	No Right Turn
No U-turn	Slippery Road	Bend to Left	Turn Left Ahead	Turn Right Ahead
Uneven Road	Dangerous Dip Road	Bumpy Road ahead	Speed Bump ahead	Tunnel ahead
No motor vehicles	Maximum Speed limit	Turn Bend	Junction Road ahead	Tunnel bridge ahead
Minimum Speed	Lane Reduction ahead	T-Junction ahead	Maximum 2 meters height	Maximum 2 meters width
Narrow Bridge	Lanes Merging Right	Y-Junction ahead	2-way traffic	Warning: Animals Around
No Parking	No Entry	No Honking	No overtaking	Railroad Crossing

How to Change a Tire

Pull Over

Pull over as far as you can if you're on the side of the road. To keep your car from rolling, the ground should be solid and level. If you're in a dark or dangerous area, drive slowly to a safer location. You may do excess damage to your rim, but you need to be safe. Call a parent immediately and let them know what is going on and follow their direction.

Turn on hazard lights

Make sure you know where the hazard light button is. It often is identified by a triangle. Set your parking brake and verify you have your hazards on. They will flash.

Get Your Tools

One thing to verify before you have a flat tire is to determine if you have roadside assistance and if your car is newer, verify if your car even has a spare tire.

Many newer cars, especially compacts, don't come with a spare tire, but often do include roadside assistance as a service.

If yours is one with a spare tire, you may also have roadside service on your insurance as an option. Check with your parents. If it's your own insurance, grab your phone and go to the insurance website or app and see if roadside assistance is part of your policy.

Assuming you're the one to change this tire, it's time to make sure you have the parts you need. You'll need a jack, wrench, and a spare tire at the very least. They should have come with your car and should never be removed from it.

Loosen the Lug Nuts

Pry off the hubcap. Secure the wrench onto a lug nut and loosen it by turning it counterclockwise. If these were put on by an air tool at a shop, they may be too tight to loosen. If you can't get them undone, calling a tow truck or flatbed truck may be your only option if you don't have roadside assistance.

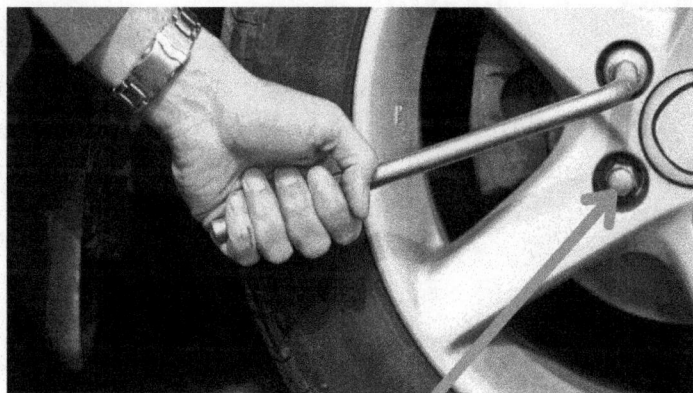

LUG NUT

Jack up the Car

Place the jack under the metal frame of your vehicle, making sure it will not come into contact with any plastic molding.

Use the jack to lift the tire you plan on changing off the ground once it's been properly placed. At all times, make sure the jack is perpendicular to the ground.

Swap Tires

If you haven't removed the lug nuts completely, do so now. Remove the flat tire and set safely aside. Put the spare on the wheel, making sure you line up the holes in the spare with the lug nut posts.

Replace the Lug Nuts

Put the lug nuts back on the spare tire. One common error with changing a tire is you may want to tighten them as you put them on. This will cause them to be out of balance. For now, just lightly hand tighten each lug nut.

Lower and Tighten

It's time to lower the car to the point that your tire is touching the ground. This will keep it from moving as you tighten the lug nuts.

Tighten the lug nuts one at a time, alternating each nut. The goal is to keep it balanced as you tighten.

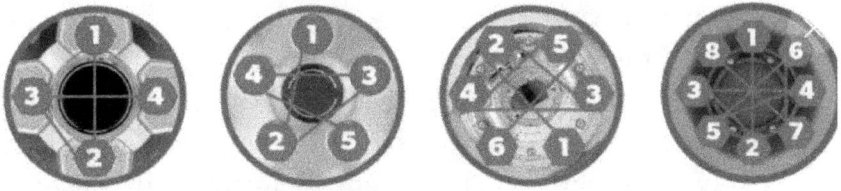

Lower and Fully Tighten

At this point, you want to lower your car completely, and begin to tighten the lug nuts completely. There is a specific tightness, or torque that should be specified for your vehicle. If you're unsure, tighten the best you can, and drive very carefully to a station and have them tighten them to the correct measure.

Stay Legal

I know this probably goes without saying, but make sure that you learn the rules and laws of driving and stay legal. For instance, driving without at least minimum levels of insurances is illegal in most states.

Additionally, if you have a loan on your vehicle with a lien holder or bank, they typically require full coverage insurance so if there's damage to the car, they don't lose their investment. Allowing your insurance to lapse/expire can force legal action to be taken against you. You might lose your license if you don't prove insurance within a specified number of days from the local government.

If you lose your license due to disrespect for the law, causing too many tickets or citations against you, you need to notify your licensing bureau to let them know that the car is no longer being driven, and even then, likely you should still keep it insured in case of unexpected damage or vandalism.

As someone who went uninsured in my younger years, when money got tight, and I had to make tough choices, the insurance seemed to be the most logical thing to cancel. It wasn't.

By going for a period of time without insurance, when I did get insurance again, the rate had increased substantially. It was only after it was too late, that I learned that insurance rates are determined based on the risk factor you, the driver, pose. If you've canceled insurance before, they assume you may do it again, and you will pay for your past decisions.

If this happens and you get a rate increase, the unfortunate reality is that you likely won't have much luck getting a dramatically lower rate with any other carrier. You'll have to shop around, compare the coverage and choose your best option, but then accept the higher rate as reality until they lower your rate in the future.

There are also annual inspections like safety inspections, emissions inspections and proof that you have paid your personal property taxes that are often associated with being allowed to register a vehicle to your name.

Even with research and a solid plan, it's common to go to the Department of Motor Vehicles (DMV) without all the right information. Do your best to go prepared because the lines are often long and it's not exactly a pleasant experience.

Once you get your vehicle registered in your own name, and you get your very first license plate, the feeling is indescribable.

You are now one major step closer to adulting. But with that title comes a lot of responsibility. Be sure you're ready for it, and don't hesitate to ask a trusted adult for help if you're not sure how to stay legal. Ignorance of the law is not a valid excuse, and it won't get you out of a ticket or a fine.

If Pulled Over by The Police

One of the things we all dread is being pulled over by a police officer. I can tell you that the police are here to protect and serve, and you should not be afraid of them.

That said, if you're doing anything wrong, it's also their job to catch you and stop you from continuing to do it. So, you're likely going to have a guilty feeling about something, even if you're not sure what you've done wrong.

The fact of the matter is if they've pulled you over, clearly, they believe you have done something wrong, or they see something about your vehicle that is concerning to them.

That doesn't mean you're going to jail or maybe not even getting a ticket, but it does mean, you need to make sure you know how to respond to being pulled over, so you don't escalate the situation.

I've been pulled over because of a taillight being out, and the officer asked for proof of insurance, which is required by law, and once he saw that, he pointed me in the direction of a nearby auto part store. Since I honestly had no idea that the taillight was out, him stopping me helped me keep myself and my kiddos safer when in the car.

If a police officer motions for you to stop or is following you while flashing their lights, stop right away wherever it is safe to do so. Unless the officer specifically asks you to exit the vehicle, DO NOT do so.

Keep your hands on the wheel and in plain sight. Keep your registration in the glove box so it is accessible and keep your license in a handy area.

Regardless of your guilt, speak with a respectful tone to the officer and understand that, like you, they're a human being, with emotions. They're not machines who love making people's lives miserable.

You'll likely come across many more great officers during your lifetime than the ones who will treat you poorly, but always be aware that you might be interacting with someone having a bad day or may not be one of the best on the force.

Without being disrespectful to the entire group, which I absolutely do not want to do, I do encourage you not to give any officer a reason to be suspicious of you or your intentions.

Remain calm, answer questions with respect, and if you're stopped with others in your vehicle, make sure you insist they behave the same way.

Sometimes people will decide they know their rights and will test the officer. The fact is some drivers and passengers may know their rights better than the officer stopping them.

Unless you are ready to take an activist-level stand, please don't escalate. Just get home safely. If you want to prove a point, do it in a safer scenario, on your terms.

Public Transportation

Commuting

In the United States, public transportation is widely used. The reason to use public transportation changes by area. In some highly populated areas, it's more logical to use public transportation over owning your own car due to the extreme traffic it would cause if everyone owned their own vehicle.

Other than traffic, for those who live in a downtown type of area, finding affordable parking for your car while you're at work is another common issue. Many who live in a suburb will drive to a transport hub and "Park and Ride" as it's often called. This saves wear and tear on your vehicle plus gets you to work without the stress of driving into the highly populated areas, not to mention the savings on parking fees.

In more rural areas, most people have their own vehicles. The traffic isn't as congested and the destinations aren't as common, making it more logical for rural residents to have their own transportation.

In moderately populated areas, busses are common. The reason for taking the bus can be diverse. Some don't have a license, a car, or simply don't want to drive when they can share a ride with others. Monthly passes are generally reasonably priced, making bus systems a decent option.

If you don't like sharing space with others, this may not be a valid option for you. Sometimes you'll sit by a talker and other times, everyone keeps to themselves. You will want to have enough social skills that you can function without fear in these situations.

Common Types in the United States:
- Buses
- Light Rail Transit
- Subways
- Trains for commuters
- Trolleys and Streetcars
- Rideshare Services
- Trams and Monorails

Travel

Traveling by Bus

Traveling from city to city or state to state by bus is very common. It's typically one of the most inexpensive methods of traveling.

Most single travelers will take a bus as it can be less expensive than driving a car. It's fairly common for minors to ride in a bus from one family member to another or for people to get to a one-way destination.

There are bus stations in most cities. This method of travel may be one that a young person would be the least comfortable with as there are stops for food and rest where you are allowed to get off the bus, and it's your responsibility to get back on in time.

Traveling by Train

While the railroad system in the United States was critical to the country's early development, it now plays only a minor role in modern transportation in the United States. Trains in the United States are divided into two categories: commuter trains and intercity trains.

Commuter trains are a type of public transportation that connects suburbs and downtown areas. Though these are not common, they provide convenient and affordable transportation throughout metropolitan areas.

Intercity trains are a type of long-distance train service that connects cities all over the United States. Amtrak operates all intercity train routes in the United States.

These trains are primarily used for leisure travel, providing scenic views of both small-town America along the journey. Sleeping cars and onboard dining are available on long-distance trains.

Train travel between cities is neither quick nor inexpensive. Most who choose trains for travel make the decision to include the travel as part of the experience.

Traveling by Plane

By far, the most common form of travel aside from personal vehicle, traveling by airplane is a popular option. The price may not be the best with short notice, but if you plan ahead, you can shop a variety of airlines from economy to first class and get to your destination much more quickly than most other forms of transportation.

Unfortunately, the United States became regrettably aware of security threats with flying, and in 2001, implemented much more stringent security requirements to board planes.

If you're flying, you should feel confident about your safety. The statistics are in favor of air travel over most other forms. The experience is typically enjoyable and even exciting.

Most people who travel on a plane are business travelers attending meetings or conventions, or families in route to a vacation destination.

Transportation Security Administration (TSA) will require you go through the checkpoint and that your luggage will comply with all restrictions. If something you have does not comply, you have the choice to relinquish it or not travel.

Wear easy to remove and slip back on shoes and research the airport requirements in advance so you are not surprised when you get through security.

Air travel is exciting, just know the rules are there to protect you.

First Aid

You've no doubt heard the expression 'Accidents happen,' right? Well, if you haven't already confirmed this to be true, I can affirm for you. They do happen; you should always be as prepared as possible for anything from a bleeding hangnail to a major laceration.

I'm not a medical doctor so using the word laceration is about as far as I'll go with using the big words. I will tell you that the internet has a wealth of knowledge on how to treat many issues or accident-related wounds. If you're ever killing time, hop onto a platform like YouTube and start searching random first aid related treatments.

I do want to be very clear though, if you are hurt in anyway, your first item on your To-Do list should be to quickly assess the situation and then determine if you should call 9-1-1, your doctor, or self-treat.

Triage is a medical term that means what I just described. In war time, they would triage those they could help from those that couldn't survive, and then they would triage down those who had minor wounds so they could care for the people who had higher need for urgent care.

Your triage will be entirely different. If something is bleeding and you can't stop it within a few seconds, you need to alert someone to help. Let them help determine if you need to call a doctor, head to the ER, or call for an ambulance.

Most accidents are minor, thankfully, and simply need to be cleaned and possibly bandaged. Having a medicine cabinet or linen closet with first aid supplies is vital for any home.

If your home doesn't have a good first aid kit yet, suggest to your adults in the home that they consider getting one.

Most families when I was growing up did just fine with a big box of Band-Aids and some antibiotic cream, peroxide, and maybe alcohol. Of course, back then, if it required anything other than that, it was assumed we were wrapping whatever was bleeding up in a towel and rushing to the closest Emergency Room.

Now, there are reasonably priced first aid kits and (again) the Internet, that just may help you avoid some trips that may have been unnecessary back in previous generations.

First Aid Kit

- Adhesive tape
- Anesthetic spray or lotion - for itchy rashes and bug bites
- 4" x 4" sterile gauze pads -for use as a soft eye patch, for dressing and cleaning wounds
- 2", 3", and 4" Ace bandages - for splinting, gauze application to wounds, and wrapping strained or injured joints

- Diphenhydramine (Benadryl) - For allergic reactions and itchy rashes, use an oral antihistamine.
- Clean/Sterile Gloves - for the prevention of infections, and they may be frozen and turned into ice packs.
- Antibiotic cream - to apply to basic or simple wounds
- Non-adhesive pads - to patch burns and wounds
- Pocket mask for CPR
- Resealable oven bag - can serve as a receptacle for hazardous items and an ice pack
- Safety pins (large and small) - to secure the triangular bandage sling and remove splinters
- Scissors
- Large Cloth Bandages - as a sling or tourniquet
- Tweezers - for splinter or stinger removal

You can assemble your own first aid kit or purchase one in various sizes with basic or extensive contents.

Remember, if in doubt, always err on the side of caution. Your parents would rather you be alive and safe even if it means having a doctor bill. All parents care about when someone is hurt is making sure they get proper attention and are safe.

If you're afraid you'll make a poor decision in an emergency, ask your parent now what they want you to do if you or someone near you gets hurt. Let them provide the emergency numbers and tell you who to call first.

Having a written emergency plan, with those numbers posted somewhere like a kitchen cabinet has saved lives and limbs. If your family doesn't have a written emergency action plan yet, suggest you create it together, and then post it for all to see.

When an emergency comes, you may not be thinking clearly, so having it written down is the way to go!

Personal Care

Personal care is exactly what it sounds like. It's the process of taking care of your grooming and other care practices that will keep you feeling clean and being healthier. Personal care is something everyone needs to understand the importance of.

For example, you need to brush your teeth regularly. The entire world tells you this, not to try to control you, but to help you learn it's a vital step in personal care that you shouldn't skip. Your teeth will literally rot and eventually, often painfully, rot out of your head.

Dental care is super important because not only does your smile open the window to your soul, but it also opens the door to friendships and relationships. It boosts your self-confidence and even though most of us are self-conscious about our appearance and our toothy grins, not having one is something you don't want to experience.

The costs for repairing all the damage of poor dental health are extreme, and many families will simply have no choice but to have teeth pulled if they can't be salvaged due to poor hygiene.

Dental care is only one example of personal care. Showing or bathing regularly is also important. Some opinions differ on if you should shower daily or less often.

I will suggest that, if your body has an odor, you should probably shower. You may need to add a body lotion if it dries out your skin. If you're not living an active lifestyle and you don't ever sweat, you may be fine with showering less often. This is preference and you should discuss it with your family as they are the best experienced at caring for the skin you're in. They literally gave it to you.

Most personal care is similar across the board, whether your body is male or female. The following tips and information are to dive in so you can choose to read the tips for the gender you associate with or are curious about. Feel free to read both, because there are areas that both will benefit from knowing about. Your choice.

Smart Brushing

I'm sure you know you need to brush your teeth. We already talked about that earlier. But there are actually smart toothbrushes out there that use an app to show you if you're reading all of your teeth or not. If brushing your teeth is a pain, try integrating a smart brush with the app to make it a bit more fun.

Something important to remember is that toothbrushes all need to be replaced at least two to four times a year. If it's electric or smart, the heads should be replaceable without having to throw out the full toothbrush.

Bad Breath

Bad breath is not only an issue for the guys. People who eat get bad breath at times. You can avoid it by cleaning your mouth and teeth of food remnants after a meal or even using mouthwash.

If you're on the go, chewing gum is a quick fix, but sometimes the choice of gum causes more issue than it helps. If you run out of toothpaste and have a crucial meeting, you can clean your teeth using with baking soda and water.

Deodorant

It's important to recognize when body odor starts to take over. You may not be aware of it, so if someone says that you stink, understand they're not trying to be hurtful or insulting, but you probably either need to put some deodorant on your armpits, or if it's been a while since you've showered, hop into the shower and clean yourself off.

Skin Care

Depending on your skin type, you may need to wash your skin multiple times a day or less often. Do your research on skin types and skin care treatments.

There are so many commercial products out there that claim to be the best. Most are fine. Some are great. But, do you know what my dermatologist suggested when I went to her with adult acne? She gave me a prescription cream and told me not to buy the pricey skin cares.

She suggested going to the local drug store and buying one of the skin care lines in the skin care aisle. She didn't say not to use the others, only that there was no reason to pay the extra costs for things that won't do any better.

I use a combination of whatever is on sale when I need it now. Don't fall into the marketing trap of needing pretty bottles or matching brands for that matter.

Yes, sticking with one system helps ensure you don't end up doubling up on some ingredients you may not need or missing out on something that could help, but you don't need to pay $40 for a cleanser when you can get a doctor recommended one for $15.

Grooming For Guys

Guys, your information is mostly the same as the girls at the core, but there may be some differences that you should be aware of.

Nail Care

Just like I mentioned to the females, it's important to keep your nails clean and trimmed properly. You want to make sure you trim any loose skin at your fingers that could cause hang nails getting caught and pulling off as well.

Where females often are expected to have longer nails, males are often expected to keep theirs shorter. This is a social norm and it helps to keep your nails at a length you can remain functional with your daily tasks.

I don't believe that you should follow a rule simply because it's a gender expectation, but you should recognize that some social norms actually make sense as well.

I've made it clear that you shouldn't care what others think, but it is commonly thought that a man with one longer fingernail may use that to take drugs. You choose what battles you want to take. I cheer you for advocating for equal rights just as I would advocate for a female demanding the same.

Some men wear nail color where many think that makes them gay or feminine. Again, if you like the look of nail color, become a trendsetter or start an awareness act as an activist.

I had a coworker who had his thumbs painted red. When I asked if it was an activist statement, he said no. His daughter painted them one day, and he liked it. So, he does it regularly now.

Did I think less of him? Nope. Sometimes it takes someone who will boldly show the world that they don't care what others think of them. He didn't intentionally set to change peoples' opinions, but in following something he liked, he opened my mind.

Do what you want. If you're not hurting anyone with your actions, dress and groom yourself to be comfortable and functional.

Problem Hairs

You may not notice it at a younger age, but sometimes your nose hairs or even hair from your ears will become unruly and grow and try to put themselves into the spotlight. Most people don't like these little pesky hairs. Get grooming scissors if you don't have an actual nose hair trimmer and tame them. You could pluck them out, but the reality is they'll show back up, and often be thicker and stronger. Trimming seems to be the best course short of going to an esthetician and having them removed with laser treatments.

You may also really enjoy having your eyebrows trimmed and waxed or tweezed. Girls are expected to avoid the unibrow, but the males get away with them being unruly. I love seeing that some guys keep their eyebrows under control. You don't have to turn them into sparkling works of art but trimmed and in control is great!

Beard Trimming

Like it or not, your face will start to grow hair. Some boys think of hair on their face as part of becoming a man. While others may dread having to spend the rest of their life maintaining hair on the one spot on their body that they can't hide.

This is often why many guys opt against trimming and maintaining at all. Currently, having a long beard is trendy, but in other decades, facial hair has shifted like regular hairstyles.

In this century alone, there was the moustache, which had its own evolution over the decades, to sideburns, clean shaven, and then the five o'clock shadow look, the nineties brought a shadow look, and the past couple decades, goatees, and full beards again. If your facial hair isn't soft, consider using a facial hair conditioner.

Your facial hair can be a great form of personal expression, or it can be a pain in the butt.

If you prefer the well-groomed look, invest in a beard trimmer and scissors to manage these hairs. One thing to consider is how your future potential mates may like—or dislike your facial hair. It's your face and hair, but if someone is going to be snuggling up to it, it's something to consider.

Shaving

If you don't want to grow a beard, you should learn how to shave properly.

Razors are now electric, water-resistant, or any other variation, demonstrating how far science has progressed.

It's no longer a total pain to lather or cream up your face and then carefully drag a sharp razor blade across your face. It can usually be managed quickly and easily if you do it daily.

If you don't have someone to help you learn how to shave, there are videos on YouTube and some shaving stores will actually help get you all set up.
Your mom may not know how to teach you, but if you're willing to talk with her about wanting to shave, I'm sure she'll bend over backwards to help you get it figured out. You're not alone!

Look in the bright side, girls get periods their whole life. You get facial hair.

Grooming for Females

Your appearance may be a big part of your life or a very small part. Either is good, as long as you are happy with how you feel about yourself. Don't present yourself in a way that others expect if it makes you uncomfortable.

Some females I know are natural beauties and barely know what skin care is, while others claim they have to work hard to be presentable enough to get out the door. – Me, I'm that group.

It took years before I realized that I didn't need to stay trendy with hair, clothes, and make up. Sometimes you may seek approval from the wrong people, and that motivates you to work harder at looking like others expect you to. Don't fall for that. Their opinions of you don't matter to your future, and if they don't love you the way you are, do you really want to be around them?

All this said to say, the below comments and tips are for personal care more than pleasing others. I encourage you to get to know who you are inside before you try to create an outside for someone else's pleasure. Live for yourself—just be clean and healthy doing it.

Hair Care

Your hair is probably something you love or hate. It's a symbol of your covering in some faiths. The care of your hair should be a priority but understand there is such a wide range of opinions on what is right, I, again, choose to suggest you talk to your parent about what they use. They are better equipped to help you with choosing the right products and knowing how often to clean your hair.

The range of conditions hair can be in often dictates how often you should wash it. If your hair is oily, you may want to wash daily. If it's super dry, you may wash every week or less often.

One caution I want you to understand. Don't judge others personal care methods compared to your own. You likely have different skin, hair, and genetics. What's a perfect plan for your body and hair may be horrible for someone else. This is a great time to remember to stay in your own lane. You do you.

If you let your hair dry naturally or use a blow dryer or styling tools, you might want to look at special treatments that will help shield your hair from the abuse (yes abuse) you put your hair through. This is me not judging your choice to abuse your hair. I've done it to mine most of my life.

Keeping up with the trends of long versus short, permed versus straight, side part versus middle, or no part at all, can become exhausting.

That said, many people feel better fitting in with others. It may make you feel like you have more in common because you look similar. You may simply like what someone else did, and so you try it too... and like it.

There's nothing wrong with keeping up with the hair trends, just be aware of why you choose the styles you do, and don't be afraid to be yourself. Be the trendsetter instead of following it every now and then.

Make Up

Back through history, people have often chosen to use color on their face to alter their appearance. Sometimes they used war paint to intimidate their enemy, others used it to try to create an appearance they did not naturally have.

There's nothing wrong with using make up. Honestly, either gender often can create a great look that's different and often attractive from their natural look. The important thing is that you use make up to create a look for yourself that you are confident and happy with.

If you want your eyes to have wings, go for it. If you want fake lashes that you can barely lift your eyes with because you have a big event and the selfies will rock with the lashes showing, grab that adhesive and go for it.

If you ever once look at the mirror and hate what you see, and feel you need to put on make up to hide the real you, then that's where I need to intervene. YOU were created in total perfection. You need to spend some time in front of your mirror, studying yourself. Look at any sags and bags, lumps, and bumps. If you look unhealthy, fix your health, don't hide the problem.

If you see a face and body that you're happy with but want to put on the make up to fit in with others, even though you don't like it... STOP.

Don't become someone else so you can fit in with others who may not yet understand what matters in life. You can be the one they learn to follow because you're more mature and get it.

Now if you want to put on makeup because your skin is blotchy and you like the way it looks better when you use foundation or concealer to level it out, do what makes you feel better.

Of course, you should also search the internet to see what makes skin blotchy and see if you might be able to just drink more water or get more vitamin C, and not need as much makeup to feel better about your appearance in the future.

Attitude about Clothes

You probably already know what I'm going to say here. You should avoid dressing to impress others as a constant mindset for your appearance. That said, clothes can make you look more organized and put together, more confident, and powerful, or on the other side, more carefree, or even more slovenly.

You should wear what makes you happy. Whether it's loose or tight (just not too tight or that can interfere with your health) if you like it; it's right!

Look at others and see if their clothes or shoe choices make them look older, younger, like they care or don't care about their appearance. Then ask yourself if you care or don't care what others think when they look at you.

Here's the thing, someone is always looking. It might be that cute guy or girl you have a secret crush on, or it could be the jerk you hate. People will judge you however their mind is set to. You need your mindset to be strong enough that you don't care what they think.

The one caution I will throw out there is try not to look like someone you aren't. I don't want to be too graphic, but if you dress provocative with low cut tops all the time, it's likely to attract the attention of those who want to see your cleavage, not you.

Their advances or harassment may be entirely unwelcomed. You have every right to wear whatever clothing you want without the fear of someone being pervy with you, but make sure you are strong in your clarity and ability to say NO, with assertion, to anyone who may like what they see when you wear revealing clothing.

I absolutely refuse to shame anyone who wears clothing that they feel great in. Just be aware that someone is always looking, and not everyone has good intentions. Stay alert, aware, and be prepared to protect yourself.

If you find that you're most comfy in leggings, sweatshirts, no makeup, and hair four-days-out from being washed, again, go for it. But consider if you're going to work or an event and consider dressing appropriately for each day and event you experience.

I'll add, as a writer, I'm often in leggings, t-shirt, messy hair, and no make-up at all, and I'm perfectly happy like this. If I go out for a book signing or event, I 'dress to impress' with comfortable, but professional clothing and enough make up, but not too much. Some days, we need to present well for others, most days, we don't have to care what others think.

Nails

Nail care should be about hygiene over appearance, but let's be real, sometimes you just want to have those long pretty nails to make you feel a boost of confidence. If it helps, go for it.

That said, you can take vitamins and keep your nails trimmed, filed, and cleaned and be just as personally satisfied. You don't have to fit anyone's expectations with your nails any more than you do with your clothes or makeup.

That said, if you choose to go with some help, do your research to know the difference between gel, acrylic, tips versus press on, and know what process should be used so that you don't get a nail fungus from someone (or yourself) accidentally letting fungus into your body.

Unwanted Hair

Let's face it, your body comes with hair in places you may not want it. Some females are perfectly happy staying au natural and leaving whatever hair in the places it grows. Others are more sensitive to removing it from places they don't feel comfortable with.

You can shave, wax, laser, and who knows what else, to remove these unwanted hairs. Some people, often depending on genetics, have more hairs showing up in places they don't want them, than others.

You may feel like it's socially unaccepted to stay natural and shave your legs, underarms, or private areas to please others rather than yourself. That's fine if that's the case. Just be open and honest with yourself about why you do it.

The good part about aging is as you get older, those hairs tend to go thinner, paler, or disappear entirely, so you might want to consider those hairs that make you feel too masculine, a sign of youth, not masculinity.

Monthly Cycles

Most females start getting their period around age twelve. It's common though for this to be as early as 8 and as late as 15. Your period is very natural, and it starts at the time you begin to ovulate.

Your body is created with many eggs from birth. As you reach a certain age, which is different for different females, your body will begin to release these eggs, usually one every four or five weeks. This is when a female body can become pregnant.

Assuming there is no fertilization of the egg as it passes from your ovaries to your uterus, the uterus will clean itself by releasing the biological matter that looks like blood and often has an odor associated with it, out of your body.

A sensitive body may feel ovulation, but many don't. However, the first day or two of your periods, you'll likely feel your body cramping as it discharges the buildup.

You may benefit from an over the counter pain reliever, heating pad, or warm bath to help with any cramping. You will become in tune with your body over time, and it's important to track your monthly cycle.

Some track it to ensure they did or did not get pregnant during the month, but even if you are not sexually active, you should track how many days your cycle usually runs and how many days your period usually lasts.

This helps to understand, so if something different pops up in your health, you'll be able to recognize the change and go to a doctor.

Not all periods are the same. Don't compare yourself if you're an early or late bloomer, and don't judge your pain tolerance to others. Each body has a different process. Some are lucky with light discomfort while others may experience intense discomfort. Going to a doctor can help pinpoint any issues as well as help get you tips on how to tolerate the inconveniences that may come with having a period.

Pads, Tampons, or Menstrual Cups

There are a variety of options for staying clean, including sanitary napkins, tampons, and menstrual cups.

Menstrual blood becomes contaminated with the body's organisms once it leaves the body. When these organisms are kept in a warm, moist environment for an extended period, they multiply and can cause urinary tract infections, vaginal infections, and skin rashes.

It is important in the case of tampons because if they are left in the vaginal area for an extended time, they can cause toxic shock syndrome (TSS). You should change tampons frequently if you go that route.

Stay Clean

While it is important to wash yourself on a regular basis during this time, all you need is some warm water to do so. You can use soap on the outside of your vaginal or vulva, but not inside.

You might get a pad rash if you're going through a period of heavy flow. It usually happens when the pad has been wet for a while and it rubs against the thighs, causing it to chaff.
Bathing not only cleanses your body but also provides an opportunity to thoroughly clean your private parts. It also aids in the relief of menstrual cramps and backache.

Use a Menstrual Cup

To get used of inserting and removing a menstrual cup may take some practice.

Inserting:

Make sure the cup and your hands are both clean. You might want to lubricate the cup to make it easier to slide in if your vagina feels dry. Fold the menstrual cup.

Take a few deep breaths and work to relax your muscles before inserting the cup. Put yourself in a comfortable position. That could be a squat while standing or a standing position with one leg supported by the toilet.

Place the cup deep enough so that no part of it protrudes into your vagina, but not so deep that you can't grasp the stem at the bottom.

The bottom of the stem should, in general, be no closer than half an inch to the opening of your vagina. If you hear a suction sound, which denotes that the menstrual cup has opened, you'll know if you inserted it correctly. To make sure there are no folds or spaces, you can also feel the cup's edges.

Try rotating the cup to make it open and form a seal if you're unsure whether it has already done so inside your vagina.

Removing a Menstrual Cup

The steps to remove your menstrual cup when it's time to empty it are as follows:

Wash your hands first. When you can comfortably grasp the bottom of the cup, gently pull on the cup's stem. To push the cup lower, you might find it helpful to bear down or tighten your abs. To break the seal inside your vagina, pinch the cup inward.

To prevent spilling any liquid, tilt the cup slightly back as you gently remove it from your vagina. Pour the cup's contents in the toilet. Before inserting the cup again, wash it with water and unscented soap.

Girls, you can stop here or keep reading what the guys have. Much of it is gender neutral.

Clothing Care

Laundry

Doing the laundry is one of those things that need to be done, but no one seems to want to do it. Truth is, as long as you know how your parents prefer it to be sorted and temperatures used, laundry is probably the simplest chore you can take on and relive some of the load for the family.

Don't overthink what each person's underwear looks like or how big or tiny they are. Just wash, fold and hang, and life will be awesome.

Sort

Here's a traditional method of sorting and temperatures if you don't have parents handy and find you need to do your own.

Some people, me included, lean toward cool/tap temperature and limited sorting at all. I might pull whites away from colors, but I've also been the type who doesn't care if my underwear are a little extra pink from something bleeding over.

• Whites go in hot, alone
• Colors go in warm with similar colors, or cold with others
• Bright colors by themselves, in cold

• Delicates should be hand washed or in a gentle cycle with cool water

Drying Time

Some people love the smell of fresh air in their clothing, so even if it seems old fashioned, some still put their clothes out on a line and let the air dry it. There's nothing wrong with doing it. It's cost efficient as well as energy efficient.

That said, what if it rains or the air is humid, and it takes a day or more to get your clothes dry? At what point, do you give up on the clothesline and throw it in a dryer?

I'm a fan of fast and easy. I like the way clothes seem softer after being in the dryer compared to a clothesline. If you prefer the smell of being out on the line, you can use fabric softener or a dryer sheet to get a nice scent to your clothes.

All this being said, it's absolutely personal preference as to how you choose to do your laundry. I'm assuming you have a washer and dryer in your home.

If you don't, going to the laundromat is a viable option. You can pay the attendant to do it for you or do it there yourself. Every now and then, it can be fun to go to the laundromat and relax and watch some tv while you wait. Most of the time, I don't allow myself time to watch TV, so it can be a nice break from daily life.

If you are without a washer and dryer at home, hand washing your personal items like underwear and anything that would be changed daily, and then drip drying them in the bathroom or outside is absolutely an option.

Iron A Shirt

It's easier to iron a damp shirt, but a good steam iron can handle a dry shirt. To avoid creasing areas that have already been ironed, follow this order. In full transparency, I'm not a fan of ironing. I buy clothes that don't need to be ironed or have them professionally cleaned because this is one of those life skills that I just never cared to learn myself.

That said, I've done the internet research for you, and these seem to be the steps that most sources agree on. I would give credit, but honestly, I scoured multiple sites so I can make sure this is accepted practice and commonly known (by most other than me, that is!)

- First step is to undo all the buttons, including the cuffs.
- Keep the iron moving, so you don't burn anything!
- It's tough to avoid creating creases. Thankfully, they're not permanent.
- Iron the back of the collar first. Turn the shirt over and iron the front of the collar.
- Next, iron both cuffs, first on the inside and then on the outside.

- The shoulders and the yoke between them. To make this easier, wrap the end of each shoulder around the ironing board's nose. Then, iron the shirt's front and back.
- The backs of the sleeves should be ironed next. Starting at the top of a sleeve and working your way down to the cuff, iron the sleeve.
- Make sure you hang the shirt quickly and lined evenly.

In case this is clear as much, check YouTube and then refer back here.

Sewing A Button

Buttons are notorious for coming off. The thread over time just gets worn and the button often pops off. You may be lucky enough to notice when it happens and save the button. They can be tough to match!

Putting a button on has a couple of processes, but honestly, people aren't going to look for a perfect thread pattern on your buttons, just get them back on, and move on with life.

If you're a bit of a perfectionist though, it's nice to know how.

1. Thread a needle, with matching thread. Tie a knot at the end where the two ends meet. You probably want about 12-18" of doubled thread to have plenty.

319

2. Push the needle through one of the tiny stitch holes where the button used to be from the *underside* of the fabric.

3. Pull the thread all the way through to the back of the fabric, where the knot will be.

4. Drop the button onto the needle and make sure you situate the button where you want it.

5. Now the fun starts. You just repeatedly stitch up and down through the holes in the button, through the clothing, and back up.

6. You should compare the other buttons thread pattern and match it. It's super simple. Is the thread diagonal or with parallel lines?

7. Continue until threads have passed through each of the button's holes four to five times.

8. Finish by tying a knot on the fabric's underside.

PERSONAL
DEVELOPMENT SKILLS

CHAPTER 4

P: PERSONAL DEVELOPMENT LIFE SKILLS

Goals

Goals are one of those things that adults probably tell you to strive for, but probably never tell you why you should care to put your effort into it.

One day, may years ago, you may have said, "I want to be a professional baseball player." And your parent probably said, that's a big goal. You'll have to work hard for that.

Of course, that'd be true, if that scenario happened, but we all know that those players come from somewhere, so every year, even if the odds are against you, if it's your own goal, you push yourself and your body harder to get better.

Then comes dating years, and going out for pizza with your friends, and you get distracted. Maybe you get out of condition and realize it's just not a realistic goal and you give up.

Sadly, most people give up on their goals and dreams much too easily. I believe the reason we give up is two-part:

1. We didn't really want it badly enough.

2. We didn't understand why we wanted it well enough.
3. They changed their mind about what they wanted.

There are entire books on this topic. I may have some if you're interested. But I do want to summarize the most important aspects that I hope will help you get and stay on course!

Get Clear

Every dream and goal should start with an EMOTION. You know the ones I keep telling you to learn to manage? Sometimes when you feel a certain way about something, you realize that this is really something you want in your life.

That's a great revelation. When grown-ups get older and responsibilities take over their lives, many of them put their dreams and goals aside. Ask your parent what their big dream or goal was, and then ask them why they put it aside.

Usually, the answer to the second question will be that they had to make a choice, or they simply changed their minds about what they wanted most.

See, this is a cycle of reality. My hope is by talking to you at a younger age, that you will never give up on your goals and dreams. You may need to adjust them, but never give up the hope/emotion and energy/effort.

Why adjust? Well, let's say you want to win the lottery. It's entirely possible, but it's out of your control for the most part and the odds are cripplingly stacked against you. Yet, people win daily. So, if that's your goal. Go for it!

If your goal is to become the next president of the United States. We've already proven that anyone can become a president, but again, the odds are stacked against you.

To reach this goal, you would need to learn the ins and outs of the political world. You would need to climb the political ladder and do great things that people follow you and support you. But, if you want to be the next president, there's probably not enough time.

So, you adjust your goal to a 10 or 20 year goal, and then it's entirely doable. Still very tough because there's only one per four years, with some exceptions, but it's possible.

Clarity is an absolute must on what you want. If you just want it in your lifetime? How will you know how to work toward it? You should choose a specific deadline or target date for the completion. If you miss it, you miss it. You can always alter, but a goal without a plan is just a wish.

You must keep track of your actions to achieve the goal. It is not enough to simply set a goal.

Action Plan

As a project manager in my corporate life, and a fixer of problems overall, my success comes heavily from creating an action plan. It's not enough to have a goal or dream. You need to create a plan that details the steps on how you can logically get there.

When you plan, you're laying out the road map for getting from where you are now to the finish line. It takes your goal from fiction to reality.

Write it Down

Write down your goal once you've decided on it. According to Dr. Gail Matthews of the Dominican University of California, simply writing down a goal increases your chances of achieving it by 42%.

Visualize it in your mind. It's there to be felt. Now, using the *S.M.A.R.T. formula*, capture it in as much detail as possible:

Be Specific

This is your goal: "who, what, when, where, and why." Describe your definition of success and the steps you're willing to take to get there.

Be Measurable

What metrics or checkpoints will you use to keep a record of your progress? For instance, if you want to save money, how much would you have to reduce your spending.

Be Achievable

Do you have the skills you'll need to succeed? If not, are you able to get them? Start now.

Be Relevant

Is this the goal you really want? Is it in line with your long-term goals?

Be Time-bound

When do you think you'll be able to achieve your goal? There is no sense of urgency without a deadline because there will always be more time. Setting a deadline encourages you to act now.

There are so many things I want to delve into with goals, but that's not the real purpose of this book. If you find you need some extra help, you can always connect with me on social media and let me know where you are with your goals.

The most important thing about goals is that you have one. I know it may seem lame, but kids become young adults, who become grown-ups. Most grown-ups give up on their dreams and goals because they felt they had to. But they didn't!

If you choose a goal from your dream, and it energizes your spirit, you need to never let that go... unless you change your mind. NOT because you need to.

Sure, you'll have to adapt and adjust as live brings more responsibilities, but never give it up. Pinky swear? ☺

Budgeting

You probably have heard the word before, but have you done a budget of your own yet? If you're not generating income, it's tough to properly do a budget, but I encourage you to give it a try with a fake job, and estimated bills, so you can at least learn how tough budgeting can be before you have to find it out on your own.

The truth about budgeting and surviving with your finances can be painful. To get loans or approved for a rental or mortgage, you must be able to prove a certain percentage of debt to income or at least an income of 2x or 3x your potential rent payment to even be approved.

Apps

There are many apps out there that help you with budgeting and tracking spending as well as your credit report. I've used Rocket Money and NerdWallet both and was happy with them.

Ideally, if you use an app, you want to be able to manually enter your income and I love the convenience of giving the app access to my bank account, so it does the hard work of tracking the money expenditures for me.

Many apps will send you regular summaries that let you know how much you're spending per week or month, and that you're spending less than you're earning, and so forth.

Many apps track if it's a recurring expense and will even remind you that a payment is coming up. It's super handy. I caution you not to rely only on the app though! Make sure you understand how to budget manually as well, because handling money is a big responsibility. You can trust technology... usually. Trust, but verify.

There are many apps out there, so search for reputable apps that are free if possible, and if you need to pay to get one you like, make sure you budget that expense as well!

Credit Score

Once the world knows you exist as a financial entity, they'll be tracking you at your level of practicing your financial wisdom.

I want you to repeat after me, "I understand that being financially responsible is vital to my entire future, and I refuse to be irresponsible with my credit for my future's sake."

Now, I'll tell you why you just had to speak that out loud. There are these groups called 'credit bureaus' and they track any credit you have, and even before you have it, they will start to track your inquiries/applications for credit.

These credit bureaus give you a score from 300 to 850, and believe me, you want to be 700+ at all times.

Anything lower, and you will be paying higher interest or being rejected entirely.

It's really unfortunate that we don't do better at teaching responsibility for your credit health like we do for heart health, but I guess people would still ignore the credit health since many of us aren't living the best heart healthy lives either.

Here's a summary of the ranges:

300-579: Poor
580-669: Fair
670-739: Good
740-799: Very good
800-850: Excellent

Any time you get an offer for a credit card in the mail or online, check the interest rate. If it's not below 20%, just throw it away.

There are many that will have cash back rewards and a zero interest rate the first year, you may or may not get the prime offers at a younger age, but hold out for a decent offer, because there are many out there that charge monthly fees and annual fees as well.

Those poor offers are the ones people who have made some bad choices with will have to accept. It's a viable way to recover your credit score if you've done some damage.

My son was given a $2,000 credit card with a very low interest rate and he's only 21 but has no verifiable employment. This could be a recipe for disaster, but we did get him this card to build his credit score, and I'm making the payments and he only uses the card as we agree.

You may want to talk to your parent about a similar arrangement to get your credit started, but understand that if you mess it up, it's your good name that is damaged, and potentially years of higher interest rates or even apartment/home or job rejections.

The 50/30/20 Rule

The 50/30/20 Rule is a simple rule of thumb budget where you estimate 50% for all your necessities, 30% for things you want, and 20% for savings and debt repayment. If you can stay in these boundaries, you're setting yourself up for success.

Now, pay special attention to that 20% though. It's savings and debt repayment, which are two very different things. I would suggest you break that down a bit further and do at 10% savings and no more than 10% debt repayment if possible.

I know I'm asking a lot once adulting starts, but while you're still likely at home and not paying rent yet, it's a great idea to save as much now as possible.

How you handle your money, and your credit score is a direct reflection on how you handle responsibility as a whole. Some will stumble a bit but get it figured out in time to stay successful. Others will stumble repeatedly until it has done enough damage that there's little hope for a full recovery.

YOU are going to be one of the greats who know how important this aspect of life is, and you're going to rock into adulting like a pro!

Decision Making

Although decision-making can be intimidating, it is much easier to deal with major decisions if you follow a few simple steps.

Nobody is born with exceptional decision making skills. It's a skill that needs to be honed and improved over the years. This means that the more decisions you make, the better you will become. It's a difficult skill to master because the better you get at making decisions, the more difficult problems you'll encounter.

Some people are apprehensive about making decisions because they are afraid of making the wrong decision. This is where decision-making begins.

Whatever you do, don't become the person who stares at a menu for twenty minutes, unable to decide. Give it a good read, ponder it a couple seconds, and then decide.

If what you got wasn't good, you can send it back for a replacement, or you can simply order something different the next time. At least you tried it and know you won't order it again, right?

Everyone wants the friend who is willing to go anywhere with them, but that doesn't mean they want you to hold back your own opinion. Don't be afraid to tell someone you prefer Pizza Hut over Dominos if that's how you feel. But, be willing to order Dominos if others want it.

One of the great things about decisions in groups is the art of negotiating and compromise. You build stronger relationships with both of these techniques.

People don't want you to be set in your ways and unwavering all the time, nor do they want you to not care about anything. They want to get to know who you are, what you like and dislike, and they want to know you're willing to flex. But, when it's their turn to flex, make sure you're ready to make a decision that you feel would be as close to a win/win as possible.

There's always a chance you'll make a 'better' or 'worse' decision when you have more than one option. Although you can anticipate where each decision will lead you, you won't know how good it is until some time has passed.

Decision Process

- What is the decision you need to make?

- What is the issue that needs to be addressed?
- What are the PROs of each option?
- What are the CONs of each option?
- What good could happen if you choose each option?
- What bad could happen if you choose each option?
- DECIDE – For better or worse.
- Evaluate initial outcome.
- Don't like the initial outcome? Change your mind if you can, or just don't repeat the same 'mistake' again.

You won't master this if you live in fear of the what ifs.

Social Etiquette

Most Common Table Settings

There are 3 most types of table settings you need to be familiar with. These are Basic, Casual, and Formal.

The types: *Basic* is what you use on an everyday basis at home unless you live with me and don't eat at a table unless you're out.

A *casual* setup is what you see in restaurants, during special occasions, and events.

A *formal* table setting is for formal dining in restaurants, hotels, etc. It's very easy to set up and identify where the utensils are.

There are more complicated setups but these three are the most common.

Basic:

- Put the placemat on the table.
- Then put the dinner plate in the middle of the setup.
- Place the napkin to the left of the dinner plate.
- Place the fork on top of the table napkin or inside the table napkin. This depends on whether you choose to fold the table napkin or not.
- With the blade pointing towards the plate, place the knife at the right of the dinner plate. Place the spoon on the knife's right side.
- Place the water glass on the upper right of the dinner plate. The location should be around 1 o'clock on the dinner plate.

Casual:

- Lay the placement on the table.
- Put the dinner plate right in the middle of the setup.
- Put the salad plate on top of the dinner plate.
- Put the small soup bowl on top of the salad plate.
- Lay the napkin right on the left side of the dinner plate.
- Put the dinner fork at the left of the dinner plate, and the salad fork to the left of the dinner fork. Place both the forks on top of the table napkin or inside the table napkin. This depends on whether you choose to fold the table napkin or not.
- With the blade pointing towards the plate, place the knife at the right of the dinner plate. Place the soup spoon exactly on the right side of the knife.
- Place the glass for water above the dinner knife.
- Place the wine glass on the right side of the water glass but place it a little bit higher.

CASUAL DINNER
TABLE SETUP

Water Glass

Wine Glass

Dinner Fork

Dinner Plate

Salad Plate

Dinner Knife

Soup Bowl

Napkin

Soup Spoon

Formal:

- Use an ironed tablecloth.
- Place the dinner plate in the middle of the setup.
- Put the soup bowl on top of the dinner plate.
- Put the bread plate at the top left of the dinner plate.
- On top of the bread plate, place the butter knife horizontally. The blade should be facing inwards towards the dinner plate.
- Put the napkin on the left side of the dinner plate.
- Put the dinner fork at the left of the dinner plate, and the salad fork to the left of the dinner fork. Place both the forks on top of the table napkin or inside the table napkin.
- With the blade pointing towards the plate, place the knife at the right of the dinner plate. Place the soup spoon right on the right side of the knife.
- Directly above the dinner plate, put a teaspoon or dessert spoon.
- Place the glass for water above the dinner knife.
- Place the White Wine glass on the right side of the water glass but place it a little bit higher.
- The Red Wine glass should be set up on top of the White Wine glass but place it a little bit to the right.
- The salt and pepper shakers should be placed on the upper portion of the dessert spoon. Salt to the left, pepper to the right.
- Place the place card in between the two shakers. The place card is an identifier for the guests and the ushers to help them find their assigned location.

FORMAL DINNER
TABLE SETUP

Salt Shaker · Place Card · Pepper Shaker · Water Glass · Red Wine Glass · Butter Knife · Dessert Spoon · Bread Plate · White Wine Glass · Napkin · Dinner Plate · Dinner Knife · Soup Bowl · Salad Fork · Dinner Fork · Soup Spoon

TIP: Whenever you're unfamiliar as to which utensil to use, just think of the "outside-in rule."

The utensils on the outside part are used first then work your way inwards. For example, if you are served salad first, then use the fork that's farthest away from your plate.

Table Manners & Proper Etiquette

Many people go through life without knowing about table etiquette. I would be one of them. If you aren't exposed to these more formal settings, it's normal that you wouldn't know how to handle yourself in this scenario.

But that's what this book is here for—to help you learn in advance, so even if you don't live in these settings, you can carry yourself with style.

If not, we've simplified the basics below so everyone would remember them when they read this guide.

Napkin Etiquette

During casual or informal meals, place the napkin on your lap. You can do this when you first sit down or as the food is served before you start to eat.

For formal occasions and locations, do not unfold the napkin yet. Wait until the hostess removes her napkin from the table and unfolds it on her lap.

Another sign is when the host or the emcee announces that "everyone can now enjoy their meal." This is because not every occasion has a hostess.

Think of a formal gathering as a bit of a symphony and you're in the strings section, watching the conductor for the body language and signs that it's time for your next action.

If you leave the table, place the napkin on your chair. After ending the meal, fold your napkin, and place it back on the left side. Go the furthest to the left if their utensils are still on the left side.

When to Start Eating

When at a small table of 2-4 people, wait until everyone has their meal before you start to eat.

For formal and business meals, wait until the servers deliver to everyone. Either that or begin to eat when the host asks you to.

For buffets, wait until the host or emcee signals everyone to start lining up at the buffet table. Follow the queue and don't cut the line.

Wait until at least 2 to 3 people have reached the table with their meal before starting.

Soup Etiquette

Dip the soup spoon sideways near the edge of the bowl nearest to you. Skim the spoon and get soup. The direction should be away from you or outwards. Sip as silently as you can from the side of the spoon.

If you want to finish the last drop of a soup, tip it away from you then similarly dip the spoon.

Cutlery Language

Did you know that your cutlery or utensils convey a message to the servers? These are then passed on to the cook or the managers. It's literally like a sign language for the kitchen and wait staff. How have we lived this long and not realized this?

Here are a few of the most common cutlery comments used in most restaurants with fine dining. Note that not all restaurants practice this but it is still good to know.

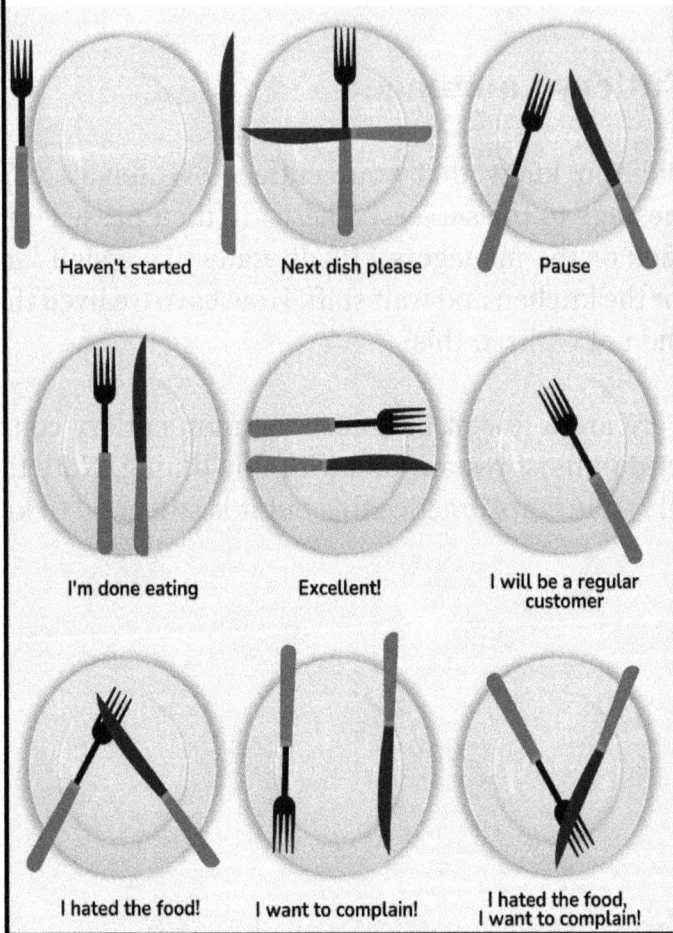

TABLE ETIQUETTE
CUTLERY LANGUAGE

Haven't started

Next dish please

Pause

I'm done eating

Excellent!

I will be a regular customer

I hated the food!

I want to complain!

I hated the food, I want to complain!

How to Host a Party

It's time to host your first party. Modern parties have a more casual vibe to them, but as you start adulting, the parties likely will become more 'proper.' Make sure you:

- Include the following information in your invitation for your guests: the date, time, location, occasion, and when and how to RSVP with your "yes" or "no." Include any additional details, such as what to wear or what to bring.
- Planning is essential.
- Even if it rains on the day of picnic or the food is a flop, a great group of people will make any party a fun and successful one.
- Prepare everything ahead of time—your meal, the table, the party space, and the refreshments—so you can relax from the start.
- Ensure that guests are greeted warmly and that they are made to feel at ease throughout the event.
- Look after each visitor.
- Correct the situation if you notice a guest with an empty glass or a single person standing alone.
- Be adaptable and gracious in your approach.
- Be the spark and the leader. It's your responsibility to run the show and notify your guests when dinner, dessert, or charades is ready.
- Circulate among your guests, introduce newcomers, and spend enough time with each group to start a conversation.
- As you say your goodbyes, thank everyone for coming.

- Don't forget to express gratitude to anyone who has given you a gift.

How to Be a Great Party Attendee

- Let your host know if you'll be there even if no RSVP is required.
- Arrive on time, but not too early. If you're going to be late, give your host an estimated arrival time so she doesn't get worried.
- Have fun like it's your job, but one you like.
- Go straight to the table when your host says it's time for dinner.
- Accept graciously and enthusiastically, regardless of how you feel, if you're asked to participate in a party game.
- Don't like to dance? Give it a try.
- When you are able, offer to assist.
- Don't eat too much.
- You should thank and compliment your host at least twice. When saying your goodbyes, always thank your hosts enthusiastically. A follow-up thank-you call the day after the party is also a thoughtful gesture. If the party was formal or given in your honor, you should express your gratitude in writing. Even after casual parties, a handwritten note or text is appreciated.

Tipping

Tipping is one of those topics that people will nearly fight about. You don't talk to friends and family about politics, religion, and tipping! Why not? Because some refuse to tip as it is currently expected. Others tip generously.

The problem is there's no solid rule book on tipping. In generations before, tipping was an amount of money given as a special thank you when someone really took great care of them.

Over the years though, in high-tip industries, people actually rely on, and are taxed on a certain level of assumed tips based off the dollar amount of the good or service they provide you.

A server used to be paid the same as, or slightly lower than, the kitchen staff. For example, kitchen staff may start at $5/hr and the server would be $3/hr. The tips would be enough to make it so a great server made more than the kitchen staff while a not-so-great server would be lucky to match the rates.

Now though, those numbers would be closer to $15/hr in the kitchen and $4/hr for the servers. It's incredibly out of balance in many industries, and the expectation is that a server will receive an average of 20% in tips. Many restaurants tax based on that assumption because some servers don't declare the accurate amount they earned.

Truly today's restaurants and other industries heavily rely on the tips to survive. The previous generations still think 10% is a good tip, and sadly, it just isn't anymore.

When and how much to tip is determined by a variety of factors, including the situation, service, and even location.

How to Tip in a Restaurant
Tipping is between 20% and 25% is recommended when dining out. If you can't afford to tip, you should go to a fast food place instead. Not judging you but think of the person on the other end as well.

How to Tip Rideshare Drivers
Tip drivers at least $2 per ride for rideshares. Many drivers average $5 per ride. Also, make sure you give them a great rating, especially if you tip on the lower end. Your ratings are almost as good as the tip itself...almost.

How Much Should You Tip in a Hotel
Leave $2 or $3 per day for housekeeping. In most hotels, the housekeeper who cleans your room one day may not be the same housekeeper the next so tip every day to be fair. This is for average rate hotels. Upscale should increase accordingly.

How to Tip at a Hair or Nail Salon
In most salons, a 20% gratuity is standard.

When in doubt, assume 20%. If their help is small, a $2 tip is a starting point. As always, hop onto your phone and do a quick search to make sure you tip well enough. But not too well!

Relationships

The word relationship can mean a lot of things. You have a relationship with your parents, boy or girl friends, and boyfriend or girlfriends. Then, you have relationships with people at work if you have a job, and anyone else you meet on a regular basis.

You rank your relationships in order of how important they are to you, which is natural. You prize the ones that make you feel the best more than likely. Again, to be expected.

I suspect, however, that you will find throughout your life that you'll have many relationships that come to mean the world to you, and you may not have even realized how important they were until they had time to develop... or they ended.

My challenge for you, overall, is to recognize the value of each person you meet. They may be serving your food, checking out your groceries, teaching you history, or someone you work with. When you meet them, think of at least one great thing about them. It can actually become fun if they're jerks. Give it a try!

Relationships are the first step to networking later in life. It's becoming a lost art in my opinion. We all call ourselves networkers because we talk nice to someone and then ask them to buy something from us. That's not really valuing the relationship though, is it?

I won't hop onto a soapbox and tell you how important it is to find greatness in others, even if they can't benefit you, but they can. The rest of this, we'll talk about how you can meet new friends. If you're not in school every day, or you don't connect with people you consider like-minded, it's important that you go out and find them where they are and create the connections.

It's so easy to think there just aren't good people or BFF material out there, but if you haven't tried, you're potentially holding yourself back from becoming part of an incredible relationship.

Train Them Well

One thing that we should all become aware of is that it's simple human nature to try to push the boundaries. We all want to know what we can get away with, and often will push that boundary to make sure it's still holding fast.

For example, if someone shows up late for work one day, they might show up in a panic, and find that the boss was pretty chill about it. So, the next time they run late, they aren't as stressed. Then, they begin to show up somewhere within the range of when they're supposed to be there.

Why? Because the manager allowed them to be late and didn't give them a consequence.

Your parents likely give you consequences for doing something against the rules, and that's why you follow the rules. If they don't have consequences, you probably don't follow many rules at all, and you either have to figure out what's best for yourself, or you might learn the hard way that making bad decisions will eventually face consequences from somewhere.

The same goes with your relationships. If you allow your friends to take you for granted, they will assume you are okay with things the way they are. It's your job to calmly describe your expectations.

So, when you start driving, and everyone always wants you to be the one driving, and paying all the gas, taking all the risks, you may want to explain your expectations, in advance.

"Look guys, I'm happy to drive, but I'll need some gas money if this is going to be a regular thing. I still have to pay for the gas, so I need some help."

Good friends will be cool with that, and you'll have set the expectation. If someone doesn't have money one time, you might say, "No worries. Get me next time." And if next time comes and they still don't have money, it will be time for you to decide if you're going to allow them to keep not contributing or respecting your boundaries.

Everyone should have personal boundaries in every relationship they have. You should follow others' expectations of you, and you should have your own

351

expectations of others. Simply put, you train others how you are willing to be treated. Don't be a jerk, but don't be a doormat.

How to Grow Your Circle

Volunteer

Find something you enjoy doing that attracts other volunteers in your age bracket or field of interest and start volunteering. You help others as you meet new people and build a network of new relationships. Ideas include animal shelters, picking up trash at parks, volunteering at community 5G walk/runs. What else can you think to volunteer that you'd enjoy even if you did it alone?

Join a League

I know bowling may seem old school, but it's also a lot of fun if you find a league that's not out for blood to win— unless you're super competitive as well. Bowling leagues and any other sports league only lasts a few months or so and then they end, giving each person the chance to join again with the same people, or move on to a different team if no special connections were built.

Sign up for Dance Classes

You might love or hate dancing, but dancing is great for your body, it gives you enough time to chat with someone without all the pressure of talking until it's awkward.

Many people are either great dancers because they practice all the time at home or social media reels, but the rest of the world is self-conscious about their lack of skills. You might meet a super special someone and have the perfect excuse for dancing cheek to cheek.

Book Clubs

Book clubs are an easy way to meet up with other readers and chat about what you thought of the recent book everyone read. These have sprung up all over the internet but are also in person.

If you don't even like reading, this may not be the best route for you, because you'll be asked to share what you thought of the book each meeting. If you are a reader though, this is a great way to meet someone you really vibe with.

Youth Groups

If you are a faith-based believer, many groups have groups specifically for the young adults of the congregation.

This an especially great option if you enjoy spending time with like-minded people of that same faith. Often, they will have field trips or other activities that make the get togethers even more fun.

The main point is that you just get out there and meet people. You're not likely to find the greatest connections next door, though sometimes you do!

How to Nurture Your Circle

When relationships are newer, they often require a bit more time and positive attention to keep them growing strong. If you like someone and want them in your life, you should remember to let them know that you like being around them.

No need to go creepy-level grateful, but make sure you casually remind them that you're glad the two of you met or became friends or whatever you feel grateful for at the moment.

You don't need to lay it on thick out of fear of them demanding the attention, because if they're overly needy, that may be a red flag anyway. Just don't forget to let them know you appreciate their friendship.

The main ingredient in a long term relationship, whether romantic or platonic is simply mutual respect, appreciation, and a level of care for each other. If you master that, you'll find a lifetime of amazing relationships, from coworkers to significant others!

Let's Dig In:

Connect

I don't just mean meet up and hang out together, though that is definitely one of the primary reasons people have friends and relationships. You want to go do fun things with others, right?

So, one of the main things that build relationships and nurture them is simply being there for each other to do fun things. It can be out and about, on social media or across a gaming system. Enjoy time with each other.

Respect

R-E-S-P-E-C-T (Did you just sing that? or do you not remember Aretha Franklin? If not, go YouTube her real quick. I'll wait...)

Respect is probably something you already do but may not even realize you're doing it. If a friend doesn't like pizza and it's your favorite food, when you're out with them, you probably don't push them to eat pizza, right? That may be a bit simplified, but at the core, you are respecting their preferences.

Another way to show respect is to listen to them when they have exciting news or had a bad day. Don't plan your next statement while you only half-listen, really truly listen.

Most of the time, friends don't need you to fix their problems, just listen to them and try to understand how it makes them feel. Some people are naturally more empathetic than others. So, if you need to spend some energy working at it, that's perfectly normal.

Much like we talked about respecting your parents, this is a similar respect. The exception is that you are sort of expected to be respectful to parents, even if you don't feel it.

Treating a friend with respect is a choice you make.

Communicate

Communication is one of those big words for another thing you already do and probably never really thought about it. You talk about classes, tv shoes, video games, and any other topics with your friends. That's communicating—verbal communication to be specific.

But here, I'm really talking about sharing thoughts and feelings. Have you ever just sat with someone, or been on the phone, and just compared your every like and dislike with each other? That sharing is something that not everyone does. You open up with people you feel connected to. Right?

If someone pours out their heart and thoughts to you, recognize that as a trust they are giving you. Obviously, you shouldn't betray that trust and you should recognize the deeper meaning.

Trust is hard to come by, but easy to destroy. If someone trusts you, unless they're doing something that puts them or someone else in danger, keep what they share to yourself.

Another form of communication, a vital one, is the one that is put in place to make sure everyone is on the same page, so there are no misunderstandings.

For example, if you have a girlfriend/boyfriend and you just decided to start using the titles, because you really like each other. The title is often assumed that there won't be more guys or girls that the new couple is going out with, or more.
But, if you don't communicate that clearly, someone may think it's no big deal to go grab dinner and a movie with someone else, leaving the other person feeling cheated on or lied to.

If you didn't communicate what being a boy/girlfriend means, it's hard to hold them accountable. You shouldn't ever assume you both are thinking the same things.

If you want strong relationships, communication is one of the top requirements.

Criticism

Let's chat about criticism and the two types. First, there's what they call *projected criticism*. This is when someone is ticked off and they blame you for the outcome. "You're a horrible friend." They might say. This is often a reactive and emotion-based criticism.

The other, better type of criticism is called *constructive criticism*. This is when someone is calm and provides you with feedback on what they think or feel you could have done differently to handle something better.

They present this in a way that it doesn't feel like an attack. It may still sting a bit, but you know they are trying to help rather than lash out at you.

When you can handle criticism between you and someone else, you can be confident that you are building a powerful relationship.

Resolving Conflicts

A fight with a friend can feel like the end of the world. You have so much connection with them, and you suddenly feel so many overwhelming emotions. Let me be clear, at any age, it can feel this way.

That's why it's important to try to avoid the fight in the first place. Not by avoiding confrontation or communication, but by having a plan in place. A process in your mind that helps you learn how to keep things from escalating, at least on your end. As long as one of you are remaining rational and calm, there's a great opportunity to avoid the knock-down, drag-out that could ensue!

See, disagreement is a healthy thing, especially between friends. You can disagree on so many things, as long as you respect your differences, and embrace the things you have in common, you're on a better track than many who have been adulting for years!

So why all the fuss, you may ask. Unfortunately, many people are so reactive with their emotions that they yell, stomp, slam, and even throw things when they feel that wave of emotion flow through their bodies.

People end up wrecking really great friendships and relationships because they don't learn how to control their actions when they're in the heat of emotions.

Work Through a Conflict

- Agree that there's zero judgement and both will let each other speak without interruption for at least thirty seconds.
- Agree that there will be no name-calling, no pointing the finger at each other or blaming and shifting responsibility.
- Agree that only topics that are relevant to the current conflict will be discussed. The only way something in the past can be brought up is if it is directly related to the current conflict.
- Agree that the person speaking, and sharing is sharing their feelings and the goal is always to work through the conflict so there is a win/win at the end, or the closest to one as possible.
- First person who brought up the conflict and wants to open it up for conversation agrees that they will explain a single scenario that made them feel a certain way.

  They will explain how that felt and explain what they hope will happen. – Often this is just to let the other person be aware they hurt your feelings, and the whole conversation can be a super quick apology and move on.
- Second person is able to share their thoughts and feelings, and the conversation should go back and forth, each listening to the other, making eye contact, even holding hands to remember that you care about the person you're having this conflict with.

- The goal is met when you both are in agreement that you each understand how the other feels and you resolve to either respect the difference while treating each other with respect, or the conflict is entirely resolved as a miscommunication or a poor action/reaction.

If you can't be productive in this effort, you may need to agree to disagree and put some distance between each other until emotions can calm down. The goal is to determine if the relationship can... or should, be saved.

Romantic Relationships

Who to Pick for Dates

Have you ever thought, "OMG, that's the person I'm going to marry one day!" based solely on what they look like, from across a room. We all have, so there's zero shame if you admit it.

But what happens when you go up to that person at a dance and ask them to dance with you, and they giggle and then turn you down? You'd probably be like, "Yeah, she's a loser anyway." Because rejection can hurt. But what can you do?

It's hard to be brave and risk rejection regardless of if you're male or female, because today, either is perfectly entitled to be the one to ask.

It's still traditional thought that the male should ask the female, but I say if you're interested in someone, do you just get over the feelings or do you get over your fears?

If your only criteria of asking someone on a date is their appearance, I will tell you this, with certainty- You're going to have a lot of first dates, and not many relationships.

You should, before you even meet someone, make a list of everything you want them to have in common with you and a list of everything that you don't want any part of in your life.

As you meet people and get to know them, see if they fall within the range of what you want in your life, to see if they have the potential to be a great match with you.

Sure, opposites attract, so they don't need to be just like you. But you should know what you really don't want to have around at all. Like, if they're a smoker, that may be on your 'dealbreaker' list, especially if you're a devout non-smoker.

Could you miss out on a great match with a dealbreaker list? Of course, but that's where timing comes in. Maybe at a later time, they will have stopped smoking and when you see them again, they now fit on your list, and you wouldn't have already dated them and broken up.

Some must haves could include:

- Nice
- Good hygiene
- Likes to smile/laugh
- Is adventurous
- Is a planner
- Is spontaneous
- Gets good grades
- Is goal driven

Some dealbreakers could include:

- Is within 0-2 or 0-5 years of my own age (This matters a lot more when you're young than when you're both 18+. I'll leave it at that, but if you're not 18 yet, you shouldn't be dating someone who's over 18... at least not yet.)

- Is a non-smoker – if they smoke, it's a deal breaker
- Does drugs
- Gets in fights
- Doesn't communicate
- Has a bad temper
- Blames everyone for their issues
- Is a cheater

As you can see, each of these two lists could go on and on, based on your own preferences.

You don't want to make it so detailed that you offer yourself no selection from those around you but be clear on what the dealbreakers are.

Sometimes you just have to take a leap and trust that there's enough emotion, or chemistry there for you to get to know each other better, and then you'll either really start to get serious, or you can end it romantically, and just move to the friend zone.

Don't be afraid of the friend zone. If you're there today, you may not be there forever. Sometimes it just takes people a while to see what's been in front of them all along. Besides, there's nothing wrong with having good friends who never become more than that. A life full of friendships is a great life lived.

Friends and Romance

If you have friends, which most people do, when you decide to start liking or dating someone. Remember that your friends are still there. It may be easy to get distracted with the newness and the whirl of emotions you feel with your new romance, but don't neglect your friends entirely.

If your romance came out of your circle of friends, nothing really needs to change. If they're addition to your circle, try to find a way to merge your circle of friends with theirs.

This is one of the biggest steps toward adulting as well. When people get married, they have to merge both their friends together as well as their families together.

If there's bad blood between any of them, it can cause drama in the bigger circle, but may also cause conflict between the two in the romance.

Not everyone has to be in your cheering section, but you may have to remove a person here and there if the conflicts cause more strain than they bring good.

Relax and Be Yourself

It's important that you each are able to feel relaxed and be yourself around each other. Sure, you should put your best foot forward, especially when going out together, but understand that your best foot still leaves the other foot that isn't shown.

If you only show each other at your best, and end up getting married, and then realize you hate how they are when they're not at their best, you may have entered into a bad situation.

That's why it's super important to allow time for each other to really get comfortable and be themselves around one another. You obviously wouldn't marry someone you think is a slob or who leaves smelly candles around 24/7 if those things were pet peeves that you have.

Abuse

Believe it or not, most abuse in the world is done by someone who claims to love or care for the people they abuse. It's not right. It's not acceptable, and if you are ever in this situation, you should tell someone right away.

Abuse can look like:

- Name calling
- Threatening
- Insulting
- Making someone feel insecure
- Treating someone with continual disrespect
- Hitting, punching, slapping, kicking
- Lack of trust
- Stalking your phone, social media

- And many other things that make a person feel bad

It can be easy to fall into an abusive relationship. The worst abusers often start out as the greatest, kindest people. Until they aren't. Once you realize they've taken that first step against you with an abusive action, you really need to step back and give serious thought to if this is something you're willing to put up with the rest of your life.

May abusers will react with violent behavior, then claim to regret it, possibly even give you a gift to apologize, and swear it will never happen again.

For some people, who made a sincere lapse of judgement or control, it might be a one-time situation. For most, it's the first of what will become a regular pattern.

If you are the abuser, you need to seriously evaluate why you lost control and ask yourself what made you feel it was acceptable to lash out and hurt someone else. If you can understand it, you can stop it—with help.

If you are the abused, you need to seriously evaluate if that person is worth bruises, broken bones, broken heart, and mind, and possibly death. Hint: The answer should be no, most of the time.

If someone is abusive and is willing to seek therapy for anger management and learn how to manage their emotions better, as long as there is a safe distance while they go through understanding emotions and acceptable shows of anger, there is hope for them and their relationships.

Never give up on yourself if you can't yet control your temper. But understand that it's not okay to lash out and hurt others with words or actions. Work on that now, so it doesn't become a bigger issue later.

There may be deeper issues that cause the abuse that really will need professional help to work through. Guess what, that's 100% the best choice. Don't bury things that hurt you. Get clear and healthy from the past so you have a great future.

One-Sided Love

Remember when I said it's important not to just date someone because of their looks? It's not because I want a lot of ugly people together. It's because you should get to know someone better, to make sure you like who they are as a person, before you let them have control over your heart.

This world is full of adults who have had their hearts broken by someone (or many someones) before the either gave up or finally found someone they could trust with their heart.

This is because in generations before, we dated based on shallow logic. Sure, you want to be attracted to the person you date, and you will! Just don't let that be the only criteria.

Imagine, you as "Sarah" out and she's polite so she says yes. You go out two or three times to movies and dinners and you really like her. She really likes going out to dinners and movies and thinks you're a really nice person, but she's just not feeling it like that.

Heartbreak story, number one. Now what do you do?

In the past, some will decide they don't care about anyone's hearts, they just are going to go out there and have fun. They got hurt, so they become the one who ends up hurting others in the future.
How sad is it that Sarah accepting a date with someone she didn't have romantic feelings for, in a roundabout way, caused the heartbreak of you, and all those others you hurt because you reacted in your heartbreak's anger?

It's absolutely vital that if you choose to date before you get to know someone very well, you hold your heart at a safe distance. You can allow yourself to feel closer to them, but don't fall in love with a stranger.

Love takes time to develop and grow. If you feel like an emotion is love in a short period of time, it's probably infatuation or something else, and maybe not real love that quickly. Or you may be falling in love with who you think they are.

What happens when you learn the type of person they really are and you don't like that person?

A heart is a very special thing that you have to offer someone. Be cautious when who you give it to. But don't live in fear of wondering if they'll hurt you. If you trust them, and know them, let that whole heart fall.

You should definitely have conversations with a romantic partner as the relationship progresses. Make sure you are both feeling the same things, or close to it. It may not always be at the same timing, but it usually works out somewhat equally.

That's why one person often knows before the other one, and then sort of waits to give the other time to catch up. That's normal and acceptable, within reason.
What you should avoid staying in, is a relationship where it's apparent that one person is in love and the other person is killing time until something better comes along.

You deserve to be the one for your romantic partner. Don't be second choice, and don't let someone else be your second choice. Release them so you can both find real happiness.

Cheaters

If you are in a relationship and find that they cheated on you, you have some grown up decisions to make. Cheating can be defined by a number of things. For this, considering your age bracket, there is a wide range of what it could mean. We'll assume it ranges from telling lies about you through going on dates with someone else.

You should verify that it's not just your suspicion, and they really did cheat on you. If so, you need to be prepared for the next action you choose to take.

You likely have cheaters on your 'deal breaker' list and should have communicated with each other if cheating is something you work through or something that ends the relationship. This is a personal decision that no one can make for you.

I wouldn't tolerate a cheater or liar in my relationships, so for me, that would be the end of the relationship. But every day, I hear of stories where someone is staying with someone who has cheated on them.

If you choose to stay with someone who treats you with disrespect and cheats on you, you may need to evaluate why you feel it's acceptable to treat you that way, and make sure you know your value.

Often, cheaters are amazing liars, and they have a way of making you feel responsible for the way they disrespect you and your feelings.

There's an expression, "Once a cheater- Always a cheater!" Ask yourself why everyone says that, and I hope you will recognize that you deserve better than being cheated on or lied to.

Try to see through that. Don't hesitate to reach out to a trusted adult or counselor if you are going through something like this and not sure how to handle it.

The Internet

Social Media Etiquette

Unless you've just climbed out of an underground bunker from the I'm going to assume that you're well acquainted with the internet and social media as a whole. In fact, I'm willing to bet you're probably more versed on the different platforms than I am.

There are so many amazing platforms out there where you can interact with others. You can share pics, stories, jokes, everything.

With the variety of people who are on the internet, it's vital that you recognize some sites are better or worse to hang out on because of the types of personalities that many on those platforms have.

For example, if you want to start a business, you might hang out on Clubhouse and listen to the channel speakers talk about their stories.

Facebook and Instagram are the long timers now. Many student-aged people have stopped hanging out there, leaving it for the adults, but that's possibly because they don't feel like they're free to post whatever they want if their parent is also on the same social media.

Before you post, keep in mind, those are human beings on the other end of the computer screen. They have feelings and just like you, they may want to just have some fun, but words can be a cruel way to have fun. Don't be the cyber bully who hurts someone else's feelings simply because you were bored.

Treat others as you would like to be treated.

Before you hit the send button, imagine how you'll feel when that person receives your message.

Apps for 16+ Only

If you're looking to get your flirt on, Snapchat and other apps house a wealth of flirty people, but remember, even if you're 16+, which is the suggested age range, what's shared there (or anywhere on the internet) can be found and shared again.

Understand that this is top on the list of not-for-kids apps. Your friends may be on these apps, but please try to be responsible as you navigate platforms.

Your parents want to give you the freedom to make good decisions for yourself, so they may choose to let you decide or they may not realize what's actually out there but try to be honest and open about what you do when you're online.

Your parent wants you to stay safe, and if they assume you wouldn't have anything to do with certain platforms, try not to disappoint them.

Open it up for conversation so they know if you're on these less-than-safe-for-kids apps and let them know what you do there. They'd rather know than be blinded by finding out after something bad happens.

If your parents ask you not to go onto certain platforms, please try to respect their wishes/rules. They only have them because there are many plots and traps out there that you may not see coming, and then end up in a really bad situation.

Dangers on the Internet

There are many traps and things on the internet where people intentionally lie to younger people with the intention of human trafficking or hurting them in some way.

If you don't personally know someone, don't tell them any personal information. NONE. There have been stories where someone will describe their front porch and their school they go to and may later talk about their dog in the yard, and that's all the bad guy needed to be able to find their house.

You may think you're being cryptic, but the people who have bad intentions out there, are tracking everything you say, and they put it all together like a puzzle, and hurting you may be their ultimate goal. Don't help them by adding more pieces to their puzzle.

I don't want to be too graphic on this, because the age range is from 13+ but please understand that there are a lot of bad people out there. They will say nice things to you to gain your trust. If they're not already friends, stay anonymous!

Catfishing

Catfishing may be a new term to you. It's when someone creates a false identity for themselves on the internet using information and images.

A catfish can sometimes steal another person's entire identity, including their date of birth, photos, and location, and claim it as their own. They then use the forged identity to persuade others to do business with them online or associate with them.

Catfishing happens a lot to people who use dating apps. To trick others into falling for romantic frauds, a catfish may pose as someone they are not.

It's important to keep in mind that not all catfish pose a danger. People catfish for a variety of reasons, including jealousy, stalking, mental instability, resentment, or a way to cheat under an assumed name. While some catfish aren't malicious, many are.

Catfish lure unsuspecting victims into believing in their false identities, allowing them to extract vital, sensitive information. Many people will ask for money right away, while others will try to obtain valuable credentials from you.

They may then use this private information for monetary gain or, in the worst-case scenario, to launch more sophisticated cyber-attacks or ransomware attacks against a company or organization you may be affiliated with. Although catfish are abundant and can have benign or evil intents, the only real method to deal with them is to understand how to avoid them.

Adult Registrations

Selective Service

When you reach the age of eighteen, you are lawfully bound, as a resident of the United States, to register with the Selective Service. This is the group who tracks all those people who were born male and residing in the US, aged 18-25.

The law specifies male persons register due to the time when only the men were fighting in wars. To date, it doesn't seem like anyone has chosen to adjust this requirement to include females.

As it relates to transgender people, those born male and transitioned to female are required to register. Those born female and transitioned to male are not required to register.

The law seems to be a bit outdated as far as equality, but as of 2022, no one has changed the way it reads.

One thing to note, even though this is required by law, registering is not the same thing as volunteering. It simply means you have acknowledged that you're a male resident and between 18-25 years old.

No one wants to go to war, and if we ever do again, I believe there would be females standing by the sides of our males. Though this is an outdated method of tracking who would be considered for a draft, there is still a process where everyone would be evaluated for suitability to be drafted.

Registered does not mean drafted! Try to consider this a part of the journey to adulthood and if you can't enjoy or be proud of it, at least recognize that there could be legal consequences if you are male, citizen of the US, and 18-25 and refuse to register.

Go to SSS.gov for more information.

Voting

Voting is one of those things that many young people take little interest in. Some, however, take a very active interest at a young age.

It's important to have a basic understanding of the government where you reside. Most in the United States, regardless of age, remain ill-informed of the specifics of the government and rely heavily on the advertising campaigns when it comes time to vote. They also rely on things like which party they belong to and who their parents vote for.

Part of the responsibility of becoming an adult is taking part in the voting process. Before you go to the voting polling location, make sure you have done more research than reading the signs along the way to the location.

I may seem to be more judgmental here than I usually am. It stems more from my personal lack of caring about politics or even understanding how the government system worked until I was in my forties.

The country will become what we allow it to become, good or bad. Yes, we have different opinions from each other, but that's the entire reason you need to vote. We will have a government where the majority of the citizens speak their voice through their vote.

There are other things, like the Electoral College, that may need to be taken into consideration as the method doesn't always indicate the majority of voters as much as a by state boundary majority.

Politics can be very interesting. Make sure you're part of the solution by educating yourself and becoming an advocate for practices that you believe in.

That said, voting is a privilege, not a requirement. You are not forced to register to vote, you are allowed to. Some people are not allowed to vote though. Non-citizens cannot vote, even if they live here. Some people with felony convictions cannot vote, nor can those who are mentally incapacitated.

Take your civic responsibility seriously and vote at each election. Sometimes it may seem inconsequential because it doesn't matter to you yet. It still should be researched and voted on, because there are times when something that sounds good has wording in it, that could be completely against something you believe in.

If they're asking you to vote your opinion, it matters enough to be voted on.

Go to USA.gov for more information about voting.

Conclusion

Getting through life is tough if you don't have a support system of great friends and family to help you through the hurdles. I intended this book to help you through any bits that you may not have covered otherwise, but don't use this book as a reason to avoid getting out there and getting to know other people.

I know it's scary at times but know there's a lot of people who felt the exact same way as you're feeling right now, and they made it through. You have had your friends and family, and now some extra HELP, so you're gonna rock this adulting thing.

Don't avoid taking the risks because the greatest rewards are on the other side of fear. Crashing through that wall where terror meets terrific is one you won't regret!

I write a lot of books for a living, and I also help people reach their writing and life goals, so if you're ever in the market to see what's involved in writing in your spare time, look me up. @JustSydneyBrown across most social media.

Oh, and make sure you hug the person who bought this book for you. They knew it was going to help. They know you're special!

Don't Forget Your Free Gift!

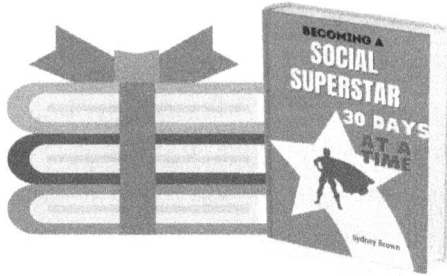

Do you feel like it's time for a change?

Are you considering moving out? Or are your parents dropping a few too many hints?

Go now and grab a free 30-day planner to get your life organized so you can get a plan together for whatever upcoming goals you have!

With this, you can keep track of:

- 30 DAY CHALLENGE
- MONTHLY BUDGET
- WEEKLY MEAL PLANNER
- WEEKLY PLANNER
- DAILY GRATITUDE LIST
- DAILY TO-DO LIST
- DAILY SCHEDULE
- DAILY JOURNAL

Go now to https://www.dontstopuntil.com/30d-ss-getyourplanner (Yes! It's totally FREE!)

TLM Publishing House

Series:

Social Stamina – 1,2,3 Let's Go!

Titles to help look at things from other perspectives and strengthen your mindset.

The Great Ascension–1,2,3 Let's Go!

Titles to help you gain focus and climb the ladder of success!

How to Start – 1,2,3 Let's Go!

Titles to help you with step-by-step, must-have knowledge of the business world and personal experiences.

Top 10 Questions to Ask Before You...1,2,3 Let's Go!

Titles with must-have questions (and logic behind) for many of life's daily and major decisions.

Social Media

Facebook: facebook.com/tlmpublishinghouse

Website: www.TTpublishinghouse.com

You can find TLM Publishing House books on Amazon and where most books are sold.

www.ingramcontent.com/pod-product-compliance
Lightning Source LLC
Chambersburg PA
CBHW071313090426
42738CB00012B/2686